Using Counselling
Skills in Social Work

Using Counselling Skills in Social Work

SALLY RIGGALL

Series Editors: Jonathan Parker and Greta Bradley

Los Angeles | London | New Delhi
Singapore | Washington DC

Learning Matters
An imprint of SAGE Publications Ltd
1 Oliver's Yard
55 City Road
London EC1Y 1SP

SAGE Publications Inc.
2455 Teller Road
Thousand Oaks, California 91320

SAGE Publications India Pvt Ltd
B 1/I 1 Mohan Cooperative Industrial Area
Mathura Road
New Delhi 110 044

SAGE Publications Asia-Pacific Pte Ltd
3 Church Street
10–04 Samsung Hub
Singapore 049483

Editor: Luke Block
Development Editor: Kate Lodge
Production Controller: Chris Marke
Project Management: Deer Park Productions,
Tavistock, Devon
Marketing Manager: Tamara Navaratnam
Cover Design: Code 5 Design
Typeset by: Pantek Media, Maidstone, Kent
Printed by: MPG Books Group, Bodmin, Cornwall

FSC

© Sally Riggall 2012

First published in 2012

Professional Capabilities Framework diagram
reproduced with permission of The College of
Social Work

Library of Congress Control Number: 2012933567

British Library Cataloguing in Publication Data

A catalogue record for this book is available from
the British Library

ISBN: 978 0 85725 840 3
ISBN: 978 0 85725 629 4 (pbk)

Contents

Series editors' preface

The Western world including the UK face numerous challenges over forthcoming years, including the need to deal with the impact of an increasingly ageing population, with its attendant social care needs and working with the social and economic implications that such a changing demography brings. At the other end of the life-span the need for high quality child care, welfare and safeguarding services have been highlighted as society develops and responds to a changing complexion. The emotional needs of individuals are often submerged within this sea of change, and demand attention to the complex ways in which social work practice must attend to psychosocial and emotional needs.

Migration has increased as a global phenomenon and we now live and work with the implications of international issues in our everyday and local lives. Often these issues influence how we construct our social services and determine what services we need to offer. It is likely that as a social worker you will work with a diverse range of people throughout your career, many of whom have experienced significant, even traumatic, events that require a professional and caring response grounded, of course, in the laws and social policies that have developed as a result. As well as working with individuals, however, you may be required to respond to the needs of a particular community disadvantaged by world events or excluded within local communities because of assumptions made about them, and you may be embroiled in some of the tensions that arise from implementing policy-based approaches that may conflict with professional values. What is clear within these contexts is that you may be working with a range of people who are often at the margins of society, socially excluded or in need of protection and safeguarding: in this book, a range of responses drawn from counselling techniques, especially from Egan's work, are redesigned for application to people marginalised within or excluded from society. This text provides an important reminder that social work represents one of the helping professions in our social world, and offers information to help you become aware of these issues, and to respond appropriately when faced with challenging situations.

The importance of social work education came to the fore again following the inquiry into the death of baby Peter and the subsequent report from the Social Work Task Force set up in its aftermath. It is timely, also, to reconsider elements of social work education as is being taken forward by the Reform Board process in England and its implementation – indeed, we should view this as a continual striving for excellence! Reflection, revision and reform allow us to focus clearly on what knowledge is useful to engage with in learning to be a social worker. The focus on 'statutory' social work, and by dint of that involuntary clients, brings to the fore the need for social workers to be well-versed in the ways in which people can be helped to engage with social work. This important book provides readers with a beginning sense of the realities of practice and the importance of understanding and applying interpersonal skills to assist people in moving forwards and/or reaching acceptance of difficult and complex situations.

The books in this series respond to the agendas driven by changes brought about by professional body, Government, disciplinary review and academic developments. They aim to build on and offer introductory texts based on up-to-date knowledge, social work and social policy developments and to help communicate this in an accessible way preparing the ground for future study as you develop your social work career. The books are written by people passionate about social work and social services and aim to instil that passion in others. The knowledge introduced in this book is important for all social workers in all fields of practice as they seek to reaffirm social work's commitment to those it serves.

Professor Jonathan Parker, Bournemouth University
Greta Bradley, University of York

About the author

Sally Riggall is a Senior Lecturer in the School of Health and Social Care at the University of Lincoln where she teaches both communication and counselling skills to social work and social care students. She is a qualified counsellor and has practised in a range of settings, encompassing doctors' surgeries and the public sector. Prior to her current position, she worked as a lecturer in further education where she managed and taught on a programme of professional counselling courses. Her research interests are primarily concerned with exploring how Egan's Skilled Helper model can assist social work students to place service-users at the centre of decision making.

Acknowledgements

I would like to thank all the students, practice educators and service-users who have so willingly given their time and contributed material to this book. I would also like to thank my colleagues at the University of Lincoln, especially Leslie Hicks and Leonne Griggs who not only shared with me their considerable knowledge and expertise but also provided me with detailed feedback and unstinting support; and Heather Flynn and Terry O'Sullivan for their kind words and practice wisdom. I would also like to acknowledge the helpful comments and advice given to me by Luke Block, Kate Lodge and Jonathan Parker at Sage/Learning Matters.

Finally, I would like thank my partner, John Conlon, for his encouragement and support. John, I dedicate this book to you.

Introduction

This book is designed to equip students and experienced social work practitioners with knowledge and skills which will help them to engage effectively with service-users. Increasingly, service-users are seen to occupy a central position in terms of practice. The personalisation agenda in health and social care, where service-users take control of their care needs and of the way these are delivered, means that helping people to identify and express their own needs is vital. Achieving this is seldom straightforward. Much relies on a high level of communication and engagement between practitioners and service-users. The skills presented in this book are designed to enable practitioners to assist service-users in expressing their needs and determining the steps which will help them to achieve change to best effect. The person-centred skills offered here are drawn from models used primarily in counselling practice. Here, the particular skills are applied to social work practice. The book uses an incremental approach where skills build on each other to provide a tool-kit of counselling skills which is tailored to use in social work.

Requirements for social work education

The Social Work Task Force Report (2010) recommends that social workers should work in a person-centred manner and help service-users to find solutions which leave them in as much control as possible. An important concept in counselling is that of believing the client is the expert on themselves and that, with focused interventions, the person can be assisted to make their own decisions, which will help them to move forward in their lives. Using counselling skills can enable social workers to assist service-users in this process.

A recurring theme in research with service-users is their desire to have social workers who will listen, respect them and place them at the centre of decision making. The Munro Review of Child Protection (2011, p25) states:

> Children have said they value an ongoing relationship with their worker, that their needs and rights to protection should be at the heart of practice, that they should have a voice, and be listened to.

The Munro Review lists core skills which are essential for social work practice. These include: conveying respect; interest; understanding; warmth; empathic concern; and being able to reflect and work with complex feelings and emotions. While few people would dispute the importance of these attributes, putting them into practice requires knowledge of *how* to do this. This book is a practical guide to developing interpersonal skills which will enable you to build effective working relationships with service-users.

Book structure

In Chapter 1 there is an exploration of what counselling skills are and why they are important in social work practice. The importance of using empathic counselling skills in engaging with service-users is established, together with an examination of skills that can help you to place the service-user at the centre of the helping process. The chapter draws on service-users' views of the skills and attributes they would like social workers to have. The Egan Skilled Helper model is introduced as a core model, which will be explored further in later chapters.

Chapter 2 investigates the person-centred skills which are essential to building meaningful working relationships with service-users. This includes the importance of non-verbal communication. The chapter explores why some service-users may not wish to engage with practitioners, together with techniques for working with people who show reluctance or resistance.

How to develop techniques of empathic responding is the subject of Chapter 3. The core conditions of empathy, unconditional positive regard and congruence, as identified by Carl Rogers, are explored, together with an analysis of the components of active listening.

In Chapter 4 there is a discussion of different levels of potential barriers which practitioners employ with service-users, including unconscious processes such as transference and counter-transference. Skills from Transactional Analysis are applied and there is a focus on self-development activities to help you to develop awareness of your own barriers.

Challenging skills are examined in Chapter 5. There is an exploration of common areas where challenging is useful, such as when people have difficulty in identifying the consequences of their behaviour. The chapter explores principles and techniques in relation to challenging, including encouraging self-challenge, identifying blind spots and working with hunches.

Chapter 6 turns to action-based counselling skills, which enable the service-user to take responsibility for decision making. The chapter focuses on how you can help the service-user to state what they need or want, set realistic and achievable goals and to identify strategies for achieving these.

The significance of loss in people's lives cannot be overstated. Chapter 7 defines different kinds of losses that service-users may experience, such as those associated with bereavement or entering residential care. The chapter identifies counselling skills which are useful both for helping people who are facing loss and when working with service-users who are nearing the end of their lives.

Working in difficult situations is often a major challenge for practitioners. Chapter 8 identifies different conflict situations and describes techniques for acknowledging and working with anger. The chapter includes how to engage in difficult conversations, such as breaking bad news. Assertiveness skills are defined and applied in different case study situations. Skills for ending working relationships are explored.

Skills learned in earlier chapters are developed and applied in Chapter 9 to working in groups. The different stages of group development are discussed, together with using skills to help groups to bond and work through difficulties. The chapter examines the use of counselling skills when working with families.

Chapter 10 summarises the tool-kit of counselling skills developed throughout the book and examines how these can be used to work with different client groups, including children, older people, those with disabilities and learning difficulties, people from different cultures and older people who have dementia. A key theme is the importance of continuing to see the service-user as a unique person.

Learning features

The book is a practical guide that will help you to engage with service-users. The importance of placing service-users at the centre of decision making is a key theme throughout each chapter. Egan's (2010) Skilled Helper approach underpins the book and is explored and applied to different social work situations. Chapters include excerpts from actual interviews with service-users, students, practice educators and practitioners where skills helpful to social work are discussed. Developing skills necessary for building effective relationships is another key area that is explored in detail. The role and importance of self-awareness is discussed and activities are presented to help you to develop knowledge of yourself. Throughout the book, case study examples and analyses of dialogue are presented as aids to learning practical counselling skills which are appropriate to social work practice. Suggestions for further reading are made at the end of each chapter.

Professional development and reflective practice

This book offers opportunities for you to learn and develop a tool-kit of skills. It is difficult to learn how to use counselling skills in social work solely by reading about them in a book. Embedding skills requires practice. I do not advocate that you should try out new skills for the first time with service-users. Instead, I suggest you practise new techniques in a safe environment where it does not matter whether or not you get it right. Engaging a classmate or colleague with whom you can try out new skills in role-play is a helpful way to begin developing your expertise. Feedback can be elicited using this method. Additionally, this enables you to reflect on your development before using newly acquired counselling skills with service-users.

This book has been carefully mapped to the new Professional Capabilities Framework for Social Workers in England and will help you to develop the appropriate standards at the right level. These standards are:

- **Professionalism**
  Identify and behave as a professional social worker committed to professional development.

- **Values and ethics**
  Apply social work ethical principles and values to guide professional practice.

- **Diversity**
  Recognise diversity and apply anti-discriminatory and anti-oppressive principles in practice.

- **Justice**
  Advance human rights and promote social justice and economic wellbeing.

- **Knowledge**
  Apply knowledge of social sciences, law and social work practice theory.

- **Judgement**
  Use judgement and authority to intervene with individuals, families and communities to promote independence, provide support and prevent harm, neglect and abuse.

- **Critical reflection and analysis**
  Apply critical reflection and analysis to inform and provide a rationale for professional decision-making.

- **Contexts and organisations**
  Engage with, inform, and adapt to changing contexts that shape practice. Operate effectively within your own organisational frameworks and contribute to the development of services and organisations. Operate effectively within multi-agency and inter-professional settings.

- **Professional leadership**
  Take responsibility for the professional learning and development of others through supervision, mentoring, assessing, research, teaching, leadership and management.

References to these standards will be made throughout the text and you will find a diagram of the Professional Capabilities Framework in Appendix 1.

Chapter 1

Counselling skills and social work

Introduction

In this chapter counselling skills are defined together with an examination of why they are important in social work practice. Research findings of the significance of empathic counselling skills in engaging service-users are discussed. Examining skills to place the service-user at the centre of the helping process is another key area of this chapter and there is a focus on the service-user as the expert on themselves. The chapter includes interviews with service-users discussing the skills they want from social workers. There is also a discussion of the compulsion social work students often feel to tell service-users what to do rather than assisting them in finding their own solutions. The Egan Skilled Helper model is a key feature of this chapter and it is discussed here together with my own research involving students from the University of Lincoln using this model during their placement.

What are counselling skills?

There is a difference between being a counsellor and using counselling skills. Counsellors undergo professional training to help people who are experiencing psychological difficulties in their lives (Nelson-Jones, 2008). Counsellors choose their training from one of the schools of counselling. The model they learn then becomes the underpinning theory by which they help clients (counsellors refer to service-users as clients). The various schools of counselling together with their individual theories can be categorised as shown in Table 1.1.

Table 1.1 *Four main schools of counselling theory*			
Psychodynamic	**Humanistic**	**Behavioural and Cognitive Behavioural**	**Systems Theory**
Sigmund Freud	*Person centred:*	Behavioural:	*Family therapy*
Carl Jung	Carl Rogers	Ivan Pavlov	*Couples therapy*
Alfred Adler	Abraham Maslow	Hans Eysenck	
Melanie Klein	*Transactional Analysis:*	B.F. Skinner	Systems theory states that individuals are all part of a wider system (e.g. families) and, as such, needs can only be addressed by working with the whole group together. This approach helps individuals to be heard and valued by other members of their group. The group leader acts as a facilitator of this process.
Erik Erikson	Eric Berne		
John Bowlby	Claude Steiner	This is more directive with different behaviours identified and goals determined. It deals with symptoms rather than underlying causes.	
	Gestalt:		
Insight is gained from exploring childhood events and phases and by understanding unconscious processes.	Fritz Perls		
	Laura Perls		
		Cognitive Behavioural:	
	These comprise a non-directive approach where power is located within the service-user. The relationship is a key element for change and this is based on respect, warmth and genuineness.	*Rational emotive therapy:*	
Practitioners try to understand events which influence the unconscious mind by recalling past incidents, interpreting dreams and helping service-users to make sense of early experiences.		Albert Ellis	
		Personal construct theory:	
	The service-user is seen as the expert on themselves and the helper's approach is to learn from them.	George Kelly	
		Both focus on changing irrational and debilitating thinking patterns.	

Each of the above schools and their associated theories involve particular skills and ways of working and counsellors would generally use the model with which they are familiar. Counsellors work in a specific way, for example holding strict boundaries by seeing a client for one hour per week and not engaging in contact at any other time. Counsellors do not act as advocates or take action for service-users. They do not engage other services (except in exceptional and serious situations), neither do they monitor people and write reports for other agencies such as courts and case conferences. The counselling relationship is a private, confidential arrangement (unless the client is threatening suicide or harm to someone else) whereas a social worker reports to their team manager and others, keeps records which may be shared with other professionals and takes an active role in doing things with and for the service-user.

Professionals from a wide range of helping professions, however, will use counselling *skills*. Egan (2010) refers to such people as 'helpers' and such professionals include doctors, nurses, youth workers, care officers, project workers, housing officers, voluntary workers and, of course, social workers. A competent social worker uses counselling skills whenever they engage with and listen to service-users; when they are establishing what the service-user needs or wants; when working with service-users who are vulnerable and in crisis; when establishing how to help or what is needed; when challenging in difficult circumstances such as in child protection and ultimately in helping service-users to change.

Social workers are not counsellors; however, a skilled social worker uses many of the skills which counsellors use in their practice (Lindsay, 2009). This book identifies these skills and explores how they are useful to engaging with service-users in social work.

ACTIVITY *1.1*

Think of a time when you needed professional help for a problem you had, for example for a medical issue. What personal qualities did you want the person to demonstrate to you? What skills did you hope they would use with you?

COMMENT

If the experience you had with the professional was positive then it is likely that they listened fully to your concerns, engaged with you in a non-judgemental manner, showed you respect and involved you in any decision-making. This kind of approach would consist of using counselling skills. A negative experience with the professional, for example where they appeared disinterested, critical or unwilling to let you discuss your issue, is likely to have left you feeling unheard, unimportant and disempowered. Counselling skills, then, involve using active listening skills, asking relevant questions, reflecting back what the service-user has implied, gently prompting and probing for more information and summarising key points made. They also involve using skills to work with reluctant and resistant service-users, challenging, managing anger, raising concerns in a respectful manner and helping people to plan and sustain action. Each of these skills will be explored in detail later.

Why counselling skills are important in social work

Counselling skills, as we have seen, constitute the building blocks of creating effective working relationships with service-users. In the review of the social work profession, The Social Work Task Force Report (2010, p21) recommends that social workers:

> *...work in a person centred manner, to support people to manage their own affairs where possible and to assist in finding solutions, which balance choice and control for the individual and their family and social networks.*

Service-users themselves clearly specify the qualities they look for in their social workers. Barnes (2002) conducted research with service-users in her report on social work education and training. She found what matters most to service-users is that social workers understand what is really happening to them and that assumptions and judgements are not made about what the service-user really wants or needs. Barnes also found service-users particularly value a high-quality relationship with their social worker. The Shaping Our Lives National User Network (cited in Trevithick et al., 2004, p21) echoes this in describing the qualities service-users seek in social workers including *warmth, respect, being non-judgemental, listening, treating people with equality, being trustworthy, open, honest and reliable and communicating well.*

The above features are all counselling skills and it is apparent that there is a strong cross-over in skills employed in counselling and those necessary to effective social work practice. There will be a thorough exploration of how practitioners can develop these skills in later chapters.

RESEARCH SUMMARY

Ethical dilemmas in learning counselling skills for social work

The reality of much social work practice in the contemporary environment is the pressure on practitioners to see ever increasing numbers of service-users in ever diminishing amounts of time. Richards et al. (2005) examine the dilemma this provokes in deciding which skills students should learn within communication skills training. Their findings are that although the pressures of practice can reduce social workers' skills to filling in assessment forms as quickly as possible, nevertheless learning to engage empathically with service-users is an essential skill to learn. It is important to understand the unique needs of every individual service-user. Richards and her team comment that skills training should focus on listening, questioning and explaining in addition to developing the use of self. Use of self means understanding our own motives and reactions in communicating with others and how these may impact on the person with whom we are engaging.

Richards and her team comment that students experience the dilemma of learning empathic counselling skills on their programmes of study only to find there is little time to practise these skills on placement. However, they comment that even though it can be challenging to make the space to use these skills, failing to use communication (counselling) skills leaves the service-user not wanting to engage at all and feeling unsupported by their social worker.

It is important, therefore, that practitioners learn, practise and use counselling skills and think about how they can incorporate these ways of working into their everyday engagement with service-users. In the course of researching students' use of counselling skills during their first practice placement, I interviewed Susan, a Practice Assessor. Susan talks about how students feel under pressure to complete assessments correctly and quickly and how, often, they simply ask one question after another. She comments:

I watch them with their heads down, intently filling in the forms, rarely looking up and with no eye contact. They are in complete control and you can see the service-user gradually sinking lower into their chair as opportunities for deeper engagement are lost. What I say to my students is, 'get to know the person, find out how they are feeling and what is happening to them. Use your counselling skills and be aware of your and their non-verbal communication. You will get all the information you need for your form by doing this. Then fill it in afterwards – in your car'.

What this experienced practitioner and practice educator is saying is yes, it is important to complete the assessment form but there is more than one way of achieving this well. As a practitioner you could read out the questions from the form one after the other and record the answers without any engagement with the service-user or you could use your counselling skills to get to know the person and their real needs and then complete your paperwork. Either way, a completed form is produced but the second method enables a much better relationship to be fostered.

In the next section, service-users and carers themselves talk about what constitutes good counselling skills.

INTERVIEW WITH A SERVICE-USER GROUP

I interviewed a service-user group that advises on university teaching, practice and procedures to find out which counselling skills they particularly value in their social workers.

Dominic: *It's nice when someone gives you a friendly smile, feeling the person is going to be friendly. It's also about giving feedback to demonstrate they have taken note of what you have been saying. It's very encouraging and it feels good to know that you have been listened to and not that the listener is assuming anything or guessing what you might be trying to say.*

William: *The first person I had, had warmth and was friendly. She was intuitive and had insight and what she did was to try to look at the positives of my life, rather than the negatives and I think that is a good thing. It puts into perspective that you have a lot of good things going for you and what you are good at. Another social worker I had was warm and kind, she listened to me well, she seemed to like the job she was doing which is a big thing. If you get the sense someone is enjoying the job they are doing, it puts you at your ease, and she put me at my ease. She was a very good listener. She seemed as though she really looked at my problem and she saw it from her side – how she would feel if she were in my situation. I have had other workers too and they were very good – they showed a lot of empathy and this helped me to build confidence because they challenged me to do things outside of my comfort zone. A good social worker has empathy and tries to put themselves in your position and see how you feel.*

Helen: *I had an involvement over a child welfare issue. It was a young guy who helped with that and it was about all of his communication skills – his body language, the way he included us in the process, the way he allowed me to read what he had written and all of those aspects that help you to trust that individual with your life, or the life of your child and that was a really good experience. The way he handled it, it was not like an official coming in, it was more like a friend, and that was really important. Trust is the first thing that happens, if you feel you can't trust someone, you've lost*

Continued

it from the beginning. He was totally open, he listened, and he came back with constructive ways to deal with the situation. The fact that he came in, had a cup of coffee, sat down and got involved with us with everyday chat just to break down those barriers – it was a pleasure to see him and get that support back.

Chana: *The professionals who have helped me have all tried their best to help me. And that has helped me – me knowing they are trying their best.*

Dave: *It has been useful when the social worker has seen what I could do and try and improve and develop those areas in a practical way. And that is how the trust is built up and I think that is quite crucial. The key to open the door is that you have got to have trust.*

Bella: *Once, a new social worker came round to see William and as soon as I met this man, I knew he wasn't going to be any good for William, and I didn't know anything about him. It was his manner and the look on his face and the way he stood. Straightaway, I knew, as soon as he walked in.*

Pam: *My bad experience with professionals is when someone came to my house and just stood there and said 'right, what is it you want?' But I have had other people who have come in and sat at my level so they are talking to me eye to eye. This is really important. And also to say back when I have said something, they have said in reply 'do I understand, you are saying...this'. That's important to me because I can then think, well, is that what I said? Or, do I need to change what I have said to get it right for me.*

Moving the locus of control from the social worker to the service-user

A clear message, then, from service-users is the need for social workers to establish good working relationships by listening and finding out what the service-user wants or needs and by being friendly, trustworthy and empathic.

Clearly there are occasions in social work where the social worker has to take charge and be directive (Lindsay, 2009). Examples include implementing court orders, removing a person to a place of safety and protecting children from harm. These instances may involve working in a way contrary to the desires of the service-user but a high level of empathic engagement skills is still required if the process is to be managed well. Using counselling skills then, can help us to work both with service-users who volunteer for services and those who are reluctant and resistant.

Social workers in training often do not distinguish easily between the skills necessary for taking direct action (for example when removing a service-user from their home to a place of safety) and those necessary for other situations such as engaging with service-users during assessments. In non-emergency situations, workers still often experience a strong desire to take charge and make things immediately better for the service-user by telling them what to do. Phrases such as *why don't you...?* or *if I were in your shoes I would...* or *have you thought about...* or *you ought to...* are common. The worker wants to feel they are helping and think this is the best way to demonstrate assistance. The following case study illustrates the importance of leaving decision making as much as possible with the service-user.

STUDENT CASE STUDY

Chrissie

Chrissie is a final year social work student. She comments on the struggle to avoid telling the service-user what to do:

> I let the service-user talk but in the back of my head sometimes I think, 'Oh why haven't you done it' because you know what might work for them but they are not in that place to be able to do that right now. But even in the back of my head, I am thinking, 'Oh God, please... just leave the relationship' but you can't say that. It is still there and I've got to do something about that. I have learned I have my own judgements in my head, I just don't impose them on the client.

Chrissie also comments on the consequences of being directive:

> I don't want to criticise, but a fellow worker has been telling her service-user what she should be doing and if she didn't do that how it was going to affect her. I think that is why the person has not engaged and it's a case of mm... 'is this another person from Social Services' type of thing.

Chrissie documents her struggle to keep the service-user at the centre of the process and encouraging her to state what she needs or wants. Chrissie is aware that what she wants the service-user to do is not matched by the service-user's desires at that moment. She also highlights how she has seen at first hand service-users withdrawing from engagement when they are directed and told what to do.

We have seen from the comments provided by Chrissie, Susan the practice educator and service-users above that taking charge and being directive when service-users are perfectly capable of making decisions for themselves prevents meaningful engagement. Indeed, the Code of Practice for Social Care Workers (General Social Care Council, 2004) states that social care workers should, where appropriate, establish the wishes and feelings of service-users and promote their rights to make their own choices and decisions, leaving them in control of their own lives.

Finding out what service-users want or need is essential, then, to engaging with people fully and promoting change. Warren (2007) comments that empowerment of service-users to take control of their own lives requires social workers to be committed to this way of working. It also requires development of a matching set of interpersonal skills. Counselling skills are the tools which can enable this to happen.

ACTIVITY **1.2**

Think back to a time when you had a big decision to make, for example changing your job, moving from one home to another or deciding what you were going to do after leaving school. Write down the choices that were available to you.

- *How did you make your final choice of what you were going to do?*

- *Did someone else tell or advise you what you ought to do?*

- *If you answered yes to the previous question, did you follow their direction? What was the outcome of this for you?*

- *If you answered no and determined yourself what to do, what was the outcome and how did you feel?*

COMMENT

Usually, if we act upon advice then this is because it matches the course of action we would have devised for ourselves. We might do as someone else suggests because we think they know better than we do. However, if we are to keep the service-user at the centre of the decision-making process, then it is important to understand that they are the expert on themselves (Rogers, 1961). Nobody understands service-users better than they do. In the above activity, nobody knew better than you what you wanted or didn't want to do. We take this for granted when we think about ourselves and it needs to become second nature to us as social care workers that we absolutely believe service-users themselves know best what they want or need.

The Egan Skilled Helper model

A useful model to learn which helps to place service-users at the centre of decision making is the Egan Skilled Helper model, devised by Gerard Egan who is Professor Emeritus in Organisation Development and Psychology at Loyola University of Chicago. Egan has written and revised his model a total of nine times but the basic premise of his work remains the same. Although it focuses on counselling, his model is highly applicable to social work and places the service-user at the centre of communication and decision making. The model focuses on developing practitioners' practical skills for engaging fully with service-users including using empathy, establishing needs and wants and identifying problem management strategies (Egan, 2010).

RESEARCH SUMMARY

Overview of Egan's Skilled Helper model

During a lecture given to Hull Cruse in 1995 Egan said the model was not his invention. He stated he had observed people successfully managing their problems and merely wrote about what they did. Egan's (2010) three-stage model can be summarised as follows:

Continued

1. What is happening to the service-user now?

2. Where does the service-user wish to be?

3. How are they going to get there?

Stage 1: What's going on now? Clarification of the key issues calling for change

In this stage, problems and opportunities are explored to enable service-users to better understand themselves. Stage one addresses what is currently happening and what prompts people to engage in social work support in the first place. This stage includes the following tasks:

1. Helping service-users to tell their stories.

2. Challenging blind spots and assisting in developing new perspectives.

3. Focusing on issues that will make a difference.

Stage 2: What does a successful outcome look like? Helping service-users to determine what they want or need that would help them

Once service-users understand their problems more clearly, they often need help in determining what they want or need instead of what they have. This stage focuses on developing a picture of a better future, choosing specific goals to work on, and committing to a programme of constructive change. Stage two focuses on the following tasks:

1. Finding out what the service-user needs or wants and assisting in identifying possibilities for a better future.

2. Helping to translate a preferred scenario into goals.

3. Assisting the service-user to commit to the goals chosen by assessing what they might need to relinquish in achieving the goals.

Stage 3: How are goals to be achieved? Helping service-users to develop strategies for accomplishing goals

In this stage, appropriate strategies are developed for achieving and sustaining goals. The tasks for stage three are:

1. Helping service-users to devise a range of strategies for accomplishing their goals.

2. Encouraging service-users to choose strategies which best fit their needs and match resources available.

3. Helping service-users to draw up and adhere to a plan of action.

The Egan model emphasises at all times the importance of service-user action and provides a framework or map for the social worker to follow when engaged in helping people. Egan (2010) draws from a number of theorists in presenting his model, including

Continued

9

RESEARCH SUMMARY *continued*

Carl Rogers' approach of building a non-judgemental relationship with the service-user by using empathy skills. However, in an interview with Sugarman (1995) Egan states that in addition to using empathy, other skills are also needed to evoke and sustain change. In stage one of his model, the service-user is listened to with empathy; challenging skills are used, again with empathy not only to help the person learn about their own ways of being but also to help them acknowledge and build on their own strengths. In stage two, a picture of a better future is identified and goals are devised with the service-user being encouraged to state what they want or need that might help them. Finally, in stage three, the service-user, with assistance from the helper, develops strategies to achieve their goals. Using the model enables the practitioner to respond empathically to service-users, challenge appropriately and find a way forward alongside placing the person at the centre of decision making.

The Egan model guides the helper through the process of engaging with service-users and also offers detailed strategies for engaging in each of the stages and tasks (Wosket, 2006). Egan (2010, p8) notes that helping is about constructive change that makes a substantive difference in the life of the client and it can be seen that this is clearly relevant to good social work practice which embraces promoting and managing change. The underlying principle of the model is that service-users know themselves better than anybody else and are therefore the experts on themselves. Social workers need to acknowledge this as the starting point to any meaningful engagement.

Understanding the service-user

Wosket (2006) emphasises a major aspect of the Egan model is the requirement to understand the service-user as fully as possible by using empathy. Empathy involves the helper trying to put themselves in the shoes of the other person and attempting to see the world through their eyes (Rogers, 1961) and this concept will be explored in more detail in Chapter 3. Wosket (2006, p14) states that helpers need to develop understanding of service-users in three ways:

1. *Understanding clients from their points of view.*

2. *Understanding clients in and through the context (the social setting) of their lives.*

3. *Understanding the dissonance wherever it appears to exist between the client's point of view and reality.*

Wosket emphasises helpers should strive to understand the individual needs of each service-user and, as such, be mindful of working with difference and diversity. In addition to this, the role of the social worker is also to help the service-user to recognise the reality of their situation. There are often times when the social worker has to gently, but effectively challenge the person, for example when the way the person sees their world is *limited, inaccurate or self-defeating* (Wosket, 2006, p14). Challenging is an essential part of social work practice and performing it well takes a great deal of practise and skill. Challenging skills will be explored in more detail in Chapter 5.

RESEARCH SUMMARY

Some of the BSc Social Work students at the University of Lincoln have been involved in a research study investigating the usefulness of the Egan model in social work settings. Most of the students quoted below are social care practitioners and released from their workplace to attend the course part-time. Here are some of their comments about applying the model to social work practice. Hollie talks about using listening skills with a family:

> With me I used the model with a whole family. I used it to help them with the current picture and moved on from there and what I found was that they all got a chance, without anybody saying anything or criticising them, to say what they felt and to just have someone there as a medium to sit and allow them to do that. It really, really worked for that family.
>
> It was quite hard for them all but I made it quite clear what we were going to do beforehand, that we were going to sit and listen to every member of the family and about how they feel and what their current picture is of what is happening now and they did all do it. And they all said afterwards that it allowed them to express what they were feeling without having that fear of somebody shouting at them because of what they felt. With one person, I paraphrased back to her what I thought she was trying to tell me and she agreed with me in the end. And she got a different view on it after I paraphrased back to her.

Hollie highlights the importance of being skilled in listening and paraphrasing. Paraphrasing means listening to what the service-user has implied from their verbal and non-verbal responses and then verbalising this back to the person. We will explore this in detail in Chapter 2. Hollie also emphasises that the family she worked with felt more free to speak openly when they realised they would be listened to without judgement. Dave discusses the importance of establishing the service-user's wants and needs:

> I think also, listening to a service-user who came to talk to the group, she said how important it was for someone to just listen and that's what she emphasised. I mean, I was quite cynical at first but yes, I have used it several time since then: it is to find out what they want.
>
> We are looking at some new projects and it seems to be imposed where we are going to do this and we're going to do that and I am saying, no, you are going to have to find out what they want and listen to what they want if you want it to work. And so it has worked that way.
>
> People have been coming from outside saying 'we are going to do this and that' and you say 'no'. It's made you think, no, you don't do that you've got to listen to what they want so we've put that into practice quite a lot. It has changed working practices really, it has. We imposed, or I imposed my own wants, I wanted them to do things, as my own values, 'you should be doing this and going there' and now I step back and find out what they want. I knew what they should be doing and am trying to think differently.

Continued

Dave documents his growing awareness of the importance of finding out what the service-user wants rather than imposing his own wants on the service-user. He realised that imposing the wants and desires of his agency took away autonomy from the service-user. He has challenged this and a different way of working has ensued. Sam works with children and families and talks about moving through the stages of the Egan model:

I started off using the first stage with children and their parents, talking to them and using empathic responses when they are upset and I've been building a relationship up with a parent to the point where in his review he pointed out he had a good bond with me and then I thought I hadn't moved on to the other stages but I have because of the things he wants. We have started with the little things and we are building up to the bigger things. The little things build onto the bigger things. It just seems to be working really well. We have been working on a couple of things and the more I do it, the better relationship we are building. It seems to be for the better really.

Sam comments on the importance of building a good relationship with service-users and how this leads to the service-user being able to state what they want or need. Heather discusses the usefulness of the second stage of the model:

I think it is a good way of engaging with people and enabling them to be involved because they have to verbally give their contribution. I think you can end up thinking up the answers yourself sometimes without giving them the opportunity. It's useful having the preferred picture because I think a lot of the time we work saying 'this is what is wrong, this is what to do' without thinking where the service-user will end up.

Heather's comment reflects many students' struggle with placing the service-user at the centre of decision making: that of finding out what is needed or wanted rather than imposing what the social worker thinks the person needs. The second stage of the Egan model is helpful in assisting practitioners to develop techniques in this area and we will explore this in more depth in Chapter 6.

Finally, Nuchjaree, a full-time final year social work student, talks about her experience of using the model during her first practice placement:

Initially using the Egan model takes more time but you move to action more quickly. With one client I worked with, the initial assessment took two hours when it is supposed to take no more than 50 minutes. But in that time I followed a hunch and said to him 'It seems that you choose to self-medicate by using alcohol'. I wondered if he would react badly to this statement but he replied, 'I think you are right, I need to see that this problem is of my own doing. I have the choice not to drink but I do drink'. He recognised the problem himself and it had more impact on him because it was his realisation. The hardest thing is getting service-users to own the problem but once you have done this a way forward happens more quickly.

Continued

RESEARCH SUMMARY *continued*

Nuchjaree found that the extra time she spent at the beginning of the process encouraging the service-user to understand more fully his difficulties produced results more quickly later on. Skills which can help people to move forward with their lives will be explored more fully in each of the ensuing chapters.

COMMENT

All of the students referred to above are experienced social care practitioners and it was interesting to find out their views on using the Egan model to engage with service-users. Together, their comments highlight the importance of establishing a good working relationship and how good, active listening is integral to this process. Using the model helped them to keep focused on the service-users' needs and to limit the imposition of their own views.

CHAPTER SUMMARY

In this chapter we have defined counselling skills as being engagement skills which are drawn from counselling theory. We have seen that these ways of working enable good working relationships with service-users to take place. We have also explored the similarities and differences between counselling and social work. While counsellors work in a contractual way with voluntary clients over a fixed period of time in a largely confidential environment, social workers operate under different constraints. Service-users may or may not be voluntary participants and consequently may be harder to engage. One of the duties of social workers is to raise concerns and to take action when necessary and such direct action is different from the role taken by counsellors. Nevertheless, there is an overlap and this chapter has begun to explore how the main concept in counselling of placing the service-user at the centre of decision making is also essential in good social work practice. Earlier in the chapter service-users have specified the engagement skills they are looking for in their social workers and we have seen how practitioners can meet some of these needs by using counselling skills. We have explored the use of the Egan Skilled Helper model as a way of placing the service-user at the centre of the helping process and seen that this model enables us to work with service-users to understand them more clearly and promote change. Practitioners and service-users' comments have concluded that the Egan model is indeed helpful in engaging service-users and we will return to particular aspects of the model in future chapters.

FURTHER READING

Egan, G (2010) *The skilled helper: A problem management and opportunity development approach to helping.* 9th edition. Belmont CA: Brooks/Cole.

Chapter 3, Overview of the helping model, pp64–90. This is a long and detailed book to which we will be returning in later chapters. This chapter gives a relatively brief and helpful overview of the Egan model.

General Social Care Council (2004) *Code of practice for social care workers.* London: General Social Care Council.

The Code reminds us of the importance of placing each service-user at the centre of the decision-making process.

Warren, J (2007) *Service user and carer participation in social work*. Exeter: Learning Matters.

Chapter 4, Empowering service-user and carer participation, pp61–78. The whole of this book is useful but this chapter in particular investigates the skills service-users seek from their social workers.

Wosket, V (2006) *Egan's skilled helper model, developments and applications in counselling.* Hove: Routledge.

Chapter 1, Background and context to the skilled helper model, pp1–29. Wosket has taught the Egan model to students at York St John College for many years. Her book explains in detail Egan's model and uses many case studies to illustrate the various stages and tasks.

Chapter 2
Building relationships

ACHIEVING A SOCIAL WORK DEGREE

This chapter will help you to develop the following capabilities, to the appropriate level, from the **Professional Capabilities Framework**.

- **Values and ethics**. Apply social work ethical principles and values to guide professional practice.
- **Rights, justice and economic well-being**. Advance human rights, and promote social justice and economic well-being.
- **Knowledge**. Apply knowledge of human growth and development, psychological, social sciences, law and social work practice theory.

See Appendix 1 for the Professional Capabilities Framework diagram.

The chapter will also introduce you to the following standards as set out in the 2008 social work benchmark statement.

5.1.1 Social work services, service users and carers.
5.1.3 Values and ethics.
5.1.4 Social work theory.
5.1.5 The nature of social work practice.
5.5.3 Analysis and synthesis.
5.5.4 Intervention and evaluation.
5.6 Communication skills.
5.7 Skills in working with others.

Introduction

Building effective working relationships with service-users is a key feature of good social work practice. Most service-users value warm, professional relationships, because in such a climate they feel able to talk about what is happening in their lives and develop the confidence necessary to manage their concerns more effectively. Service-users describe good relationships as being those in which they feel respected, listened to and understood by their social worker. In this chapter, service-users talk about the relationship skills they seek from their social workers and how respect, empathy and honesty enable trust to develop and change to take place. Core requirements necessary for the practitioner to build constructive relationships include a desire to understand service-users' difficulties and the ability to work in a non-judgemental way while being genuine, open and honest during interactions.

The very first contact between the social worker and service-user is important because it can determine the whole path of the work undertaken together. The importance of verbal and non-verbal skills are explored in building relationships and these are broken down into techniques which can be learned and practised. However, while these skills are the building blocks of good relationships, the glue which cements their foundations is the practitioner's demonstration of genuineness and a heartfelt desire to get to know the service-user. This chapter explores the use of various theories including Rogers' (1961) core conditions. The chapter also draws from Egan (2010) in describing how service-users can be reluctant or resistant to engage and examines ways in which the social work practitioner can work with hesitant or averse service-users.

Why it is important to build relationships with service-users

If social workers are going to be able to help service-users, the very first requirement is to form a good working relationship. Indeed, Nelson-Jones (2008, p28) writes *connection is the essential requirement of any relationship.* Good relationships enable trust to develop and also encourage service-users to work together with the social worker in managing problems. Gilbert et al. (2008) researched the importance of the relationship in mental health care and found that good relationships are characterised by workers who use active listening skills to engage with service-users. Borg and Kristiansen (2004) also conducted research with recipients of mental health services and found that service-users are more likely to recover when practitioners work with them in collaborative partnerships, and demonstrate empathy, respect, good listening skills and a willingness to focus on service-users' priorities. Both of these studies show that the quality of the relationship between the helper and the service-user is a key factor in helping to assist in managing problems.

Carl Rogers was one of the founders of the person-centred approach. His theory postulates that service-users are the experts on their lives and that the quality of the relationship between the helper and service-user is the key to change. The worker needs to be able to take the lead from the service-user in finding out what would help or assist them the most. Rogers (1961) believed that forming a therapeutic relationship with the service-user makes it easier for them to communicate. Rogers states that the helper needs to sensitively understand how service-users see themselves and to understand their perceptions and feelings without being judgemental towards them.

One of the key aspects of Rogers' person-centred way of working is that a relationship where the helper is open and honest and listens non-judgementally to the service-user is enough on its own to evoke change. Rogers (1961, p22) comments:

> The more I am simply willing to be myself, in all this complexity of life and the more I am willing to understand and accept the realities in myself and the other person, the more change seems to be stirred up. It is a very paradoxical thing – that to the degree that each one of us is willing to be himself, then he finds not only himself changing; but he finds that other people to whom he relates are also changing.

Rogers is saying here that, in building a relationship, the role of a helper (in our case the social worker) is to enable the service-user to feel comfortable talking about what is really going on for them. By talking through problems and issues in a climate of trust, acceptance and good listening skills, service-users will begin to gain greater insight into their situation. From this heightened understanding, the person will then be able to devise changes to their lives which would help them better manage their problem situations.

Nelson-Jones (2008) also comments on working co-operatively with service-users. He states that people will collaborate with helpers if they feel understood and where goals are mutually decided rather than imposed.

Skills in building relationships with service-users

The attitude of the social worker

The approach and attitude of the social worker is very important in establishing good working relationships. The helper needs to demonstrate acceptance of the service-user as a unique human being (Rogers, 1961) and to believe wholeheartedly in people's rights to express their own thoughts and feelings (Nelson-Jones, 2008). Wishing to explore these concepts further, I conducted an interview with Faye, who is a single parent with five children. She is a service-user who copes with a progressive physical disability. In the following piece she talks about what she values most in the relationship with her social worker and how the attitude of the worker is important from the very first moment.

CASE STUDY

Faye says of her social worker:

I would be gutted to lose her. I think the sun shines out of her and she really has brought me on. The first time she came to see me she blustered in, dumped this bag in the middle of the floor and said, 'Can I use your toilet?' And all of a sudden she went from being this woman who was going to walk in with a clipboard being this person who was all-seeing, all-knowing, all-qualified, and to tell me I couldn't cope, to being human. Because at the time, in my head, if I couldn't work out why I couldn't cope, I couldn't see how anyone who was supremely qualified to run a family could walk in and see how I would be able to cope. If I couldn't see, how could they? We had a cup of tea, we talked, she listened. I know she listened because when she came back again she was asking me if anything had changed and how I felt about what we talked about last time. And it wasn't the Spanish Inquisition: we talked, almost like friends, not quite but almost. She made herself very approachable. I had a big image of what a social worker would be: someone with a matronly image that would bustle in and tell me what I should be doing, or tell me that I couldn't do what needed to be done, my ultimate fear being that they would take the children away. And she was none of those things. She was really human, really approachable. I expected her to come in with a list of questions and go tick, tick, and be more clipboard than person. But she was very much a real person and chatty and I learnt a little bit about her as well – only a little but enough for me to know she was human and to feel she felt comfortable with me. I felt like a door opened, it was a two-way relationship, she was a professional doing a job but I didn't feel there were any judgements. It felt as if she was as comfortable with me as I was with her, and that made a big, big difference.

Faye's message is clear: the attitude of the social worker is crucial to the quality of the helping relationship. Nelson-Jones (2008, p62) comments that *good beginnings increase the chances of good middles and good endings*. The social worker's attitude at the first meeting therefore influences the whole period of time spent with the service-user. Faye tells us how important it is for the social worker to establish a good working relationship from the very beginning. She highlights the importance of feeling comfortable with her social worker and how experiencing the worker as another human being helped her to feel more relaxed and able to talk. She talks openly about her fears that the social worker would treat her as a 'task to complete' and then proceed to take over her life by telling her what to do. She also expected and feared being judged for her difficulties in coping. What helped her most of all in that first meeting was that the social worker engaged with her on an equal level as one human being to another. By her actions, the social worker made it clear she wanted to get to know Faye and find out what was happening in her life without judging her in any way. The effect of this approach on Faye was that a weight was lifted from her shoulders because she could honestly share what she was finding difficult.

ACTIVITY **2.1**

Imagine you are a service-user who is finding it difficult to cope. You finally decide to seek some help and now your new social worker is visiting you at home.

- *How would you want the social worker to be with you?*

- *What could the social worker do that would help you to feel more comfortable in speaking about yourself?*

- *What would put you off from engaging with the social worker?*

COMMENT

This activity helps you to place yourself in the shoes of the service-user at the point of first contact with a social worker. It is likely that if we were seeking help we would be feeling vulnerable and fearful of being judged. We need to recognise how challenging it may be for the service-user to put their trust in us.

The core conditions of a helping relationship

Carl Rogers believed that developing a good relationship with a service-user is not only a means to helping a person to manage their difficulties but also an end in itself. What Rogers (1961) means by this is that creating a warm, empathic, non-judgemental and trusting relationship where the service-user is upheld as a unique human being will be enough for the person to grow and change. Rogers writes about three 'core conditions' as being important in developing the relationship. These are unconditional positive regard, empathy and congruence. Empathy is where we try and put ourselves in the shoes of the service-user and attempt to understand what it is like for them (Rogers, 1961). Empathy is explored more fully in Chapter 3. In this chapter, we will define and explore unconditional positive regard and congruence.

Unconditional positive regard

From the moment we are born, we seek approval from our caregivers. We wish to be loved, respected and accepted as unique individuals in our own right (Hough, 1998) and this desire usually continues throughout our lives. Rogers (1961) writes about the importance of conveying warmth to service-users, that is to say demonstrating that we respect and care for the person we are working with. He states that in a climate of warmth and understanding, the service-user can feel accepted and more able to trust their helper. Beresford et al. (2008) conducted research with service-users facing life-limiting diseases and carers facing bereavement. The team found that the vital qualities service-users value most are kindness, compassion, sensitivity, empathy, caring, thoughtfulness and warmth. Defining what warmth towards others looks like is not easy, although we know instinctively how we feel when others are expressing warmth to us. The following approaches can demonstrate warmth:

- Smiling when it is appropriate.

- Leaning forward towards the service-user.

- Using appropriate facial expressions which reflect the emotions described by the service-user.

- Listening and demonstrating that you are listening.

- Showing that you are trying to understand what the person is telling you.

- Displaying that you too are a human being, for example by using humour if this is applicable to the situation.

Expressing warmth, however, is much more than the sum of its parts. Thinking mechanically before your visit *I must smile appropriately, and lean towards the person...* will not automatically mean you are expressing warmth. The key stream which must flow through your entire engagement is a genuine interest in the service-user and a wish to get to know and understand them. You need to be yourself, relax and be willing to learn from the service-user. Remember they are the expert on themselves and will be teaching you about their lives and circumstances. On some occasions, being genuine and warm can be a challenge for us, such as when the service-user has engaged in activities which we find abhorrent. For example, you might be working in a prison setting with a man who needs services and who has convictions for child sexual offences. Maintaining unconditional positive regard does not mean we have to like the person or agree with his view of the world. Rather, it is important to see him as a person with individual needs and to focus on these rather than concentrating on past activities.

ACTIVITY 2.2

Ask two colleagues, friends or fellow students to work with you in a trio (three of you together). Ask one person to talk to you for five minutes about an issue they wish to explore. Ask the other person to act as your observer. At the end of the session, ask the observer to give you feedback on how you demonstrated warmth with the speaker. Find out from them exactly what you did, or did not, do.

The word *unconditional* in relation to positive regard means accepting the service-user without evaluation or judgement. We can see what Rogers means by this when we look again at Faye's comments from earlier in this chapter. Once she experienced her new social worker being non-judgemental towards her, she was able to relax and talk openly about her situation.

Of course, one of the roles of social workers is to make judgements of situations and the difference between making judgements and being judgemental is not to be confused. For example, in child protection work a judgement may need to be made regarding whether or not a child is meeting development milestones or whether neglect is an issue. However, once this kind of judgement has been made, the raising of the concern is best achieved by using a non-judgemental approach with the service-user. This is illustrated in the following case study.

CASE STUDY

Let us suppose that Jodie, 21, is the mother of two-year-old Freddie. Jodie has suffered from an eating disorder in the past although she is no longer receiving treatment. Twice a week Freddie goes to a child minder and this person has raised concerns because Freddie often seems hungry and sometimes tries to take food from other children's plates during mealtimes. The health visitor also is concerned that Freddie is underweight for his age and suspects that Jodie is not feeding him enough. The social worker visits to undertake an assessment, and finds that while Jodie is providing three meals a day for Freddie, she is mainly feeding him thin soup. The social worker makes a judgement that this is insufficient food for Freddie to thrive. She therefore has to raise this concern with Jodie.

If the social worker was to raise the concern without any consideration of unconditional positive regard, she might use the following tone with Jodie:

> Jodie, you are not looking after Freddie well enough. If you don't start feeding him properly we may have to take him into care.

A better approach, which demonstrates respect and warmth to Jodie, would involve the social worker taking the time to find out what is going on in Jodie's life which results in her only preparing soup for her son. The social worker might say:

> Jodie, I can see how much you love Freddie but I have to tell you that I am concerned that Freddie is underweight for his age. I know this is a difficult area for you but I am here to help you find ways to improve things.

Approaching the service-user with as much understanding as possible, as illustrated in the second example, helps the person to feel understood, accepted, cared for and supported. Likewise, the service-user is much more likely to engage with the social worker and change her behaviour if the social worker adopts a warm, empathic and supportively challenging approach.

Accepting the service-user without being judgemental also means holding back from making positive judgemental comments. Rogers (1961, p55) writes:

Curiously enough, a positive evaluation is as threatening in the long run as a negative one, since to inform someone that he is good implies that you also have the right to tell him he is bad.

Rogers states that the more we hold back from making any kind of judgemental statement of the service-user, the more the person will evaluate themselves. This will increase their self-responsibility and independence. The service-user will move towards making judgements for and about themselves, rather than waiting for and responding to the evaluation of another.

RESEARCH SUMMARY

A writer who demonstrates the importance of remaining non-judgemental during deeper therapeutic work is Virginia Axline, a child psychologist. In her book, Dibs, in search of self, *Axline (1964, p46) documents progress in engaging with and helping a young boy called Dibs to develop his confidence. In one session Dibs paints a picture in the playroom. He refers to Axline as 'Miss A':*

As he added more colours the picture emerged. When he had completed it, he had a painting of a house, a tree, sky, grass, flowers, the sun. All the colours were used. There was in the finished painting relationships, form, and meaning.

'This is … This is…Miss A's house,' he said. 'Miss A, I'll give you this house.'

'You want to give me that do you?' I said, gesturing towards his painting. He nodded. The purpose of this response, rather than an expression of thank you and praise, was to keep our communication open and to slow it down. Then, if he wanted to, he could add more of his thoughts and feelings and not be abruptly cut off by my response and involvement and values or standards of behaviour.

It would have been easy for Axline to say 'Oh, thank you Dibs, that's lovely'. This would have been a judgemental comment (albeit a positive one), the underlying message being you have pleased me. *However, by choosing not to give praise and instead reflecting back the feeling behind Dibs' gesture (Dibs' desire to give Axline a gift), this enabled Dibs to remain in touch with his own developing sense of self.*

Of course, this is an example of working in an advanced and highly therapeutic way with a child who is still growing and learning. In the course of more usual interactions, for example working with people who have low self-esteem and who often feel worthless, it is important to help them to develop self-worth. We can do this by using lots of encouragement and helping the person to recognise their successes and developing strengths. Our feedback needs to be sincere as well as honest and this approach (congruence) will be explored later in this chapter.

Engaging in a truly non-judgemental manner is difficult to achieve but nevertheless a constant aim in building relationships. Try the following activity to gauge how far you are along the spectrum of being truly non-judgemental.

ACTIVITY **2.3**

Imagine you are working with the following service-users. How easy would it be for you to remain non-judgemental in your thinking and approach?

1. *Michael, 56, is unemployed and seeking help for alcohol dependence. He is unkempt, smells and has clearly been drinking when he sees you. He tells you that although he is signing on for benefits, he gets paid work 'on the sly' and is proud that he never has to pay tax.*

2. *Andrew, 49, is a pillar of his community. He is a local businessman and heavily involved in a local charity which raises money for people who have multiple sclerosis, a condition his wife Anne suffers from. Andrew is the main carer for Anne. You know from your involvement with Anne that Andrew is frequently verbally abusive towards her. They have no children and Anne does not wish to leave Andrew.*

3. *Priscilla is 28, was born into a wealthy family and is dependent upon prescription drugs. She was educated at an expensive private boarding school and she speaks with an upper-class accent. She expresses extremely racist and homophobic views to you about her neighbours during her interaction with you.*

4. *Abi is 17, a single parent who is struggling with her two children, a two-year-old daughter and a one-year-old son. Two months ago she began a new relationship and is now pregnant again.*

5. *Monty is 82 and experiencing increasing levels of memory loss. He lives in sheltered accommodation and keeps getting lost when he leaves his house. He knows his name but cannot remember where he lives. He has been independent all his life and is desperate to remain where he is rather than go into residential care, which his daughter is suggesting.*

Congruence

Congruence can be defined as being open, honest, sincere and being the real you with the service-user. Rogers (1961) states that for the service-user to experience their helper as being truly trustworthy, the helper has to be able to communicate their feelings and perceptions honestly and accurately. Rogers writes that when we are feeling annoyed or exasperated with the service-user, if we do not recognise this in ourselves then it will be portrayed in our body language, facial expressions and often in our verbal communication. If we are being congruent, then first we need to recognise and then express what is going on for us openly. In other words, Rogers is stating that we need to be *real* with the other person. Being real strengthens the relationship because it means we are not hiding behind a professional façade. Wearing a professional mask leads us to think *'how should I be behaving'* rather than *'what is truly going on for me in this instant'* (Nelson-Jones, 2008).

Thorne (1990, p117) describes this as forging a relationship *without pretence and without the protection of professional impersonality*. Thorne states that congruence can be demonstrated by displaying our true feelings: letting the service-user see we are emotionally affected when they are telling us something very sad is being congruent. Being real, then, enables us to meet the service-user as one human being to another.

CASE STUDY

Faye, the service-user we met earlier, tells us how she values the honesty, or congruence of her social worker:

It's not about her being infallible because I'm really comforted by the fact that she is human and not omnipotent. She says to me, 'I don't know, but I'll find out and ring you back' and she does. She treats me with respect. She treats me like an equal. She does not look down on me. She is realistic: if it can't be done she will tell me. When I haven't known what I've needed, she has sat down with me and narrowed down options of what is realistic. She is brilliant.

It is clear from Faye's comments that she values the honesty her social worker brings and this has strengthened Faye's trust in the relationship. Understanding clearly what the social worker can and cannot do enables Faye to operate within the parameters available to her.

ACTIVITY 2.4

Ask someone who knows you well and who will give you objective feedback to help you work through the following questions:

1. *Briefly describe how effective you are in establishing good working relationships with people.*

2. *What do you do best in establishing and maintaining working relationships?*

3. *What do you need to do to become better at establishing and maintaining good working relationships with others?*

COMMENT

As we have seen so far in this chapter, being skilled in establishing and developing working relationships with service-users is not simple or easy. Neither can it be achieved without a high level of self-awareness regarding our own motives and judgements. Engaging another person to give us honest feedback helps us to develop our own self-knowledge and enables us to work on our skills.

Non-verbal communication

Developing awareness of our non-verbal communication

Verbal communication skills, as we are seeing, are very important to establishing relationships with service-users. How we communicate non-verbally is equally as important. Our facial expressions, body language and our proximity to service-users all tell people, albeit unconsciously, what we are really thinking and feeling. Returning to Rogers' (1961) points made earlier, if we are genuinely interested, respectful and striving to be non-judgemental, then our body language is far more likely to demonstrate openness, warmth and acceptance to the people with whom we are working.

Many writers have documented the importance of non-verbal communication. Caris-Verhallen et al. (1999) for instance, found that non-verbal behaviours such as nodding, leaning forward and eye contact were important in establishing good relationships. Egan (2010, p133) writes that *clients read cues in your nonverbal behaviour that indicate the quality of your presence to them.* By this, Egan means that service-users continually assess whether or not their helper is trustworthy enough to open up to. For example, glancing at your watch can convey that you are thinking about being somewhere else. Folding your arms may occur because you are feeling cold or because this is something you do naturally but we need to be mindful that the service-user may interpret this as a sign that you are withdrawing your interest.

Egan (2010, pp134–36) gives guidelines for *visibly tuning in* to service-users by suggesting the following 'SOLER' framework:

- **S** Face the service-user **squarely**. This means demonstrating that you want to listen and are giving the message that you are there for the person. Sitting absolutely squarely may be a little threatening so instead try placing your seat at a 45 degree angle to the speaker. This enables the person to feel you are engaging with them without pinning them down with no escape.

- **O** Adopt an **open** posture. This means that you need to convey to the service-user you are not feeling defensive towards them and are open to their communication. You would do this by uncrossing your arms and legs. If you are a natural leg crosser and it is difficult for you to refrain from doing this, at least make sure you cross your legs towards the person rather than away from them.

- **L Lean** towards the speaker. Doing this indicates to the person that you are interested in what they have to say. You need to be careful not to lean forward too far and invade the speaker's personal space. In this instance it would be better and less invasive to move your chair back before leaning in towards the service-user. Neither should you lean back away from the person. Doing this will make you appear bored or disinterested.

- **E** Maintain good **eye** contact. This means maintaining steady eye contact with the speaker rather than staring. Not everybody finds it easy to look someone directly in the eye and if this applies to you then focus somewhere in the triangle between the speaker's eyes and their mouth. This gets easier with practice and demonstrates to the speaker that you are interested in what they have to say. You also need to be mindful of cultural differences regarding eye contact. Members of some cultures may find it difficult to give and receive this. Egan states that when working with a service-user who is visually impaired, eye contact is still important to maintain because you will then be aiming your voice and body language towards the person. The person will then sense this and know you are attending fully to what they are saying.

- **R** Try to be **relaxed** and natural. This means not fidgeting, or playing with items such as your pen, or fiddling with your hair. Keep your hands still and try also to keep your facial expressions calm and relaxed.

This checklist is easy to read and remember; however, it is difficult to actually embrace fully and employ these skills well. The key point to remember is that you need to be *genuine* in your commitment to engaging with the service-user. You are there to learn from the other person and, as such, your full concentration is required. If this attitude remains at the forefront of your practice then you will use SOLER skills without being consciously aware that you are doing so.

ACTIVITY 2.5

This activity is influenced by an exercise suggested by Egan (2010, p134).

Sit in a public area where people are seated together such as a refectory, café, park, etc. Identify two people who are deep in conversation and listening to each other. Make sure you maintain a respectful distance (you are not there to eavesdrop on what is being said) and just observe the non-verbal behaviour of each person while they are listening.

- *Keep Egan's SOLER checklist in front of you.*
- *Assess whether the listener is sitting squarely to the speaker, adopts an open posture, leans towards the other person, maintains eye contact and appears relaxed.*
- *Observe the effect these skills have on the speaker.*
- *Finally, practise SOLER yourself with someone next time you have a conversation and assess the effect this has on the person who is engaging with you.*

Observing and working with service-users' non-verbal communication

Observing the service-user's facial expressions and body language can indicate to us how they might be feeling inside. Koprowska (2010, p12) writes that *emotion is felt, expressed and seen in the body*. This means that verbally someone can say one thing, such as *'yes, I'm fine thank you'*. However, the person's body language may indicate that they are feeling anything but fine. Koprowska writes about the importance of unravelling any incongruence between what the service-user is saying and how they are appearing non-verbally. Woodcock Ross (2011) also states it is very important for the social worker to recognise incongruence between verbal and non-verbal behaviour. She states a service-user might, for instance, be afraid to explore a particular area for fear of the consequences. They might then verbally appear to engage with the social worker about the topic while at the same time non-verbally demonstrate they are feeling uncomfortable. For example, a person might speak quite calmly and matter-of-factly about their partner's violence towards them saying they can cope with his outbursts while simultaneously displaying a clenched jaw, no eye contact and tapping fingers and feet. An observant social worker will first notice and then tentatively explore this with the person.

In the next section, we will explore this concept further in assessing how to work with service-users who find it difficult to engage.

Working with reluctant and resistant service-users

Reluctance

Service-users become involved with social workers for a variety of reasons. Some people look forward to their engagement with practitioners and see from the outset that the relationship will be fruitful and helpful. Examples here might include a couple who wish to adopt or foster a child and know they will be proving their competence, or a person who has a physical disability and wants a social worker to help them arrange direct payments for care. Another group of people presenting for help might be classified as *reluctant* service-users. Reluctant service-users know they need help but may not know how to ask for it or feel shame or embarrassment about their problem. According to Egan (2010) many people are reluctant to engage because the mechanics of change are difficult and challenging. They may feel shame or have lost hope that things can change for the better.

Avis et al. (2007) conducted research within Sure Start centres to establish why some people are reluctant to engage with services available there. They found that participants: experience difficulty in asking for help; sometimes feel fraudulent in accepting help; lack confidence to ask; fear the authority of staff; sometimes do not trust staff and other parents they do not yet know and fear getting into conflict situations. Many find it difficult to admit needing help with parenting, feeling a sense of shame that they are struggling. In building relationships with service-users, practitioners need to be mindful that it is often difficult for people to seek assistance, even when help is desperately needed.

Other reasons are discussed by McKelley (2007) who researched why some men are reluctant to engage in mental health services. He found that ways in which men are socialised can leave them reluctant to express their emotions, afraid to admit weaknesses or vulnerabilities and feeling they ought to be able to solve problems on their own. He found some men see it as a weakness to seek help from others and, in some cases, their sense of their own masculinity is challenged because they do not feel in control: something they have been brought up to expect. Again, as practitioners we need to try and put ourselves in the shoes of each individual service-user and try and see what it is like for this particular person to be seeking help.

Resistance

While reluctant service-users want to engage without necessarily knowing how to, resistant service-users do not wish to have involvement with helpers because they feel coerced (Egan, 2010). As such, they are harder to make relationships with. Resistant service-users often think they are mistreated by social workers. According to Egan, they can let everyone around them know they definitely do not need any input from helpers and may sabotage any assistance offered. Behaviour can range from passive non-participation to outright belligerent or aggressive and abusive conduct. Examples of resistant service-users include people referred by court order (e.g. for compulsory treatment) and parents under investigation for child protection matters. Another example is a son or daughter who believes their parent should be placed in residential care and who resists attempts to provide a package of care enabling the older person to remain in their own home. It is also important to remember that some service-users will be resistant due to their previous experiences with a range of people (especially those in authority) and this may have affected their trust in professionals. People who have been subjected to discrimination may also find it difficult to trust helpers and therefore display resistance.

Working with reluctant and resistant service-users

The first stage in working with people who are both reluctant and resistant is to recognise that these traits are present and to be expected in many cases. Egan (2010) offers a number of strategies for working in this area.

RESEARCH SUMMARY AND CASE STUDY

Egan's (2010) approach to working with reluctance and resistance

Egan gives a number of suggestions for helping reluctant and resistant clients in a counselling relationship. Here we will apply his principles and then, using examples, show how they are applicable in social work settings. Let us imagine Jenna is a social worker who is making an assessment at the home of Melanie, the 22-year-old mother of five-year-old Aaron. Aaron's school has made a referral because he is turning up to school hungry and tired and often falls asleep in class.

- *Explore your own reluctance and resistance: identify areas in your own life where you may be reluctant or resistant to engage with another person. Think about what has helped you to engage in the past and draw on this to help you in your practice. For example, Jenna identifies that as a teenager, when her mother forced her to do something, she would react by just digging in her heels because she felt coerced. Now, as a social worker, Jenna understands that if she forcefully tells Melanie what to do, she herself is likely to encompass resistance because Melanie will experience her as being more powerful.*

- *See some reluctance and resistance as normal: this involves recognising that Melanie might well feel shame when the social worker appears at her door and questions her parenting skills. She may worry as to whether her neighbours notice the visit. At the very least, showing resistance demonstrates that Melanie is feisty and has spirit. These traits will help Melanie later if they can be channelled into a more purposeful direction. For example, if Melanie shows resistance to social work involvement this could be interpreted that she is fighting to keep her child.*

- *See reluctance as avoidance: this means recognising that change may be difficult for Melanie because she does not know where to start in making things better. She loses sight that she could gain control of the situation so tries to avoid it by keeping her head down and hoping nobody will notice things are going wrong. A way forward is to gently help Melanie learn different ways of managing the situation.*

Continued

- *Accept and work with reluctance and resistance and examine the quality of your interventions:* now she knows these are normal, Jenna will be ready to experience a reaction from Melanie. Jenna needs to acknowledge Melanie's resistance, for example by saying: Melanie I can see how hard this is for you to have me visit because you feel I am questioning your ability as a parent. And I think you might be afraid I am here to take Aaron away from you. *It is important for Jenna to recognise the difficult feelings Melanie might be experiencing towards her and to work through these, listening without judgement.*

- *Establish a 'just society' with the service-user:* this means Jenna needs to acknowledge and deal with Melanie's feelings of coercion by maintaining respect for her and, where possible, sharing the planning of any action. Jenna needs to invite Melanie to participate in a way forward, to share her expectations of Melanie and elicit Melanie's expectations of her. This honest sharing of the difficult feelings they both have in this situation can enable trust to develop and a way forward to be found.

- *Help the service-user to search for incentives for moving beyond resistance:* helping Melanie to identify what is in her own self-interest is one way of encouraging her to participate. Although she is struggling to be a good enough parent to Aaron, it is clear that Melanie is finding it hard to put into practice what she needs to do. Jenna is more likely to overcome Melanie's resistance by identifying a course of action which will also help Melanie. She could say something along the lines of: Melanie, I can see you are really struggling to do all the things you need to do for Aaron at the moment. For one thing, I know it's hard for you to get him to bed on time and this must be exhausting for you because you won't be getting any time to yourself at all. I can help you to develop some strategies which will help you to do this. *Egan states an important incentive is for the service-user to realise she can remain as much as possible in charge of her own life.*

- *Engage significant others to help and, later, employ the service-user as a helper:* it could be that the service-user will respond to being helped by other people. Melanie might be willing to let her family assist her or to attend parenting classes. At a later date, she may be willing to help other parents facing difficulties. Avis et al. (2007), in their research with Sure Start centres, discovered parents find it easier to accept help from other parents in the programme and value staff giving advice while they are playing with their children or in discussion groups without ramming it down their throats. The team also found that where the participants are then able to help other parents, this helped their own self-confidence.

CHAPTER SUMMARY

In this chapter we have seen that building relationships needs to be at the forefront of social work interaction. Service-users tell us that the attitude of the practitioner matters from the very first moment of contact and that both the verbal and non-verbal communication portrayed by the social worker is crucial in establishing a trusting relationship. For change to take place, service-users need to know their helpers are going to value them as unique individuals, remain non-judgemental, be open and honest and strive to see the world from their perspective. We have explored how difficult these concepts can be for the practitioner to employ well. We have also seen how, ultimately, it is when the service-user and practitioner work together as one human being to another that change is achieved and sustained. We have also explored how and why many service-users are either reluctant or resistant to work with professionals and how this can be seen as normal behaviour given the circumstances in which social workers appear in people's lives. If practitioners can acknowledge to service-users why they might be angry or scared to engage and find ways of working with and overcoming this, then the developing quality of the relationship will give the best possible chance for change to take place.

FURTHER READING

Avis, M, Bulman, D and Leighton, P (2007) Factors affecting participation in Sure Start programmes: A qualitative investigation of parents' views. *Health and Social Care in the Community*, 15 (3): 203–11.

This is a very interesting and readable study of what helped participants in Sure Start services to engage with services, workers and other parents.

Axline, V (1964) *Dibs, in search of self*. London: Penguin.

This book demonstrates the person-centred relationship building skills of the author who documents working with a little boy who would not talk or play. I, and everyone I know who has read it, found this book impossible to put down.

Egan, G (2010) *The skilled helper: A problem management and opportunity development approach to helping*. 9th edition. Belmont CA: Brooks/Cole.

Read the section entitled 'help clients manage reluctance and resistance', pp116–26. This is situated in Chapter 4. Also, the section on non-verbal behaviour and the SOLER technique is useful on pp132–35.

Chapter 3
Empathic responding

A C H I E V I N G   A   S O C I A L   W O R K   D E G R E E

This chapter will help you to develop the following capabilities, to the appropriate level, from the **Professional Capabilities Framework**.

- **Values and ethics**. Apply social work ethical principles and values to guide professional practice.
- **Knowledge**. Apply knowledge of human growth and development, psychological, social sciences, law and social work practice theory.
- **Critical reflection and analysis**. Apply critical reflection and analysis to inform and provide a rationale for professional decision-making.
- **Intervention and skills**. Use judgement and authority to intervene with individuals, families and communities to promote independence, provide support and prevent harm, neglect and abuse.

See Appendix 1 for the Professional Capabilities Framework diagram.

The chapter will also introduce you to the following standards as set out in the 2008 social work benchmark statement.

5.1.4 Social work theory.
5.1.5 The nature of social work practice.
5.5.4 Intervention and evaluation.
5.6 Communication skills.
5.7 Skills in working with others.

Introduction

One of the key requirements that service-users frequently express is the desire to feel understood by their social worker (Barnes, 2002). Therefore, it is highly important that social workers try and understand what service-users are feeling and experiencing. Demonstrating this understanding is called empathic responding. This chapter defines what empathy is and explores why it is such an essential skill in social work when working with service-users. The importance of developing a full understanding of service-users' thoughts and feelings is discussed together with a detailed exploration of a range of empathic responding skills. The requirement for social workers to be clear and honest in their communication is also considered by exploring the use of assertiveness skills within empathic responses. To become skilled in empathic responding takes more than learning and applying a set of techniques. It also requires a real desire to understand the service-user at a deep level and this chapter explores some of the challenges in developing and using high-level responding skills.

What is empathy?

Carl Rogers (1902–1987) was an American psychologist who was integral in developing the person-centred approach to working with service-users. His theory assumes that no one understands the service-user as fully as the service-user does. Rather than the helper or anyone else being an expert on the service-user, he or she is seen as the expert on themselves. Rogers' belief was that each of us is made up of two parts. The first is an organismic self, consisting of that part of us which is who we really are, and the second is a self-concept, which comprises the way we have adapted to how others want us to be (Rogers, 1961). The following case example explores the relationship of these two concepts.

CASE STUDY

Rosemary

Imagine you are working with Rosemary who tells you that she is thinking of going into residential care. If Rosemary had fully considered the implications of such a move and decided that this is the best option for her and something she really wanted for herself then this choice would be coming from her organismic self. However, Rosemary might have a daughter who has been telling her that 'going into a home would be for the best because you would be looked after and would not have to worry any more'. *Rosemary might then still say to you that* 'it would be best if I went into a home' *because she had let herself be persuaded that this is the right course of action. She might also want to please her daughter at the expense of what she really wants, which is to stay in her own home. In this instance, Rosemary's self-concept would be in operation.*

The purpose of using empathic responses with Rosemary is to help her uncover her organismic self, her true self and to establish her real feelings. Thorne (1990), in writing about Rogers, comments that the self-concept is heavily dependent on the attitude of people who are significant others in the service-user's life. Deci and Ryan (2002) write that the organismic self and self-concept are not easily separated because a healthy personality is characterised by creating close relationships with others and that this involves responding to their needs too. If people surrounding the service-user are judgemental and quick to make assumptions about them, then they can rapidly lose sense of their organismic self as their self-concept takes over. Taking time to get to know Rosemary and to really listen to what she is both saying and not saying would be the first step in being empathic and to help her to establish her organismic self and thus her true feelings. Once the service-user's real feelings and desires have been established it enables them to choose a course of action which is truly desired (Rogers, 1961). In Rosemary's case, the social worker in recognising what she really wanted would then know how to help her.

Rogers (1961) defines empathy as the attempt at stepping into the shoes of the other person and trying to see their world as they might see it. Empathy involves trying to understand what the person might be feeling and experiencing and Rogers states it is this process, the striving to understand that is crucial. In the case of Rosemary, the social worker would need both to listen and observe her body language and facial expressions when she is talking about going into care to establish what her real feelings are. Working in a person-centred way and attempting to be empathic means asking oneself the following question, *Can I let myself enter fully into the world of the client's feelings and personal meanings and see them as he or she does?* (Rogers, 1961, p53). What is important here is that social workers are able to recognise the true feelings of the service-user in this situation. This will help the person to keep in sight what they really want. Of course, goals will need to be assessed for how realistic and achievable they are but the starting point is always to begin with the service-user's wants or needs.

A common fallacy is to believe that empathy consists of how *you* would feel if you were in the same situation as your service-user. However, you need to be able to distinguish between what the service-user's feelings might be in their particular situation and what *your* feelings would be if *you* were in this situation (Mearns, 1997). You are not the service-user and remember, the service-user is the expert on him/herself. We will explore this concept more fully later in this chapter.

Why using empathy is important in social work practice

Social workers who use empathic responding skills in the course of their communication are quite rare. Forrester et al. (2008) found that most social workers do not use empathy. Instead, they found the most common type of verbal communication is to ask a series of questions, usually one after another, and that social workers are fifteen times more likely to use a questioning approach rather than an empathic response.

While many skills of social work and counselling overlap, in some areas social work is distinctly different (Lindsay, 2009). One factor that sets social work apart from counselling is that the role of social work is to raise concerns and to take action when necessary. Forrester and his team researched the effects of using empathic responses in raising concerns in child protection cases. They found that social workers in child protection teams who are skilled in using empathic responses get parents to disclose more information about difficulties in their family than social workers who lack these skills. They also found that using empathic responding skills is essential in maintaining good working relationships with parents after they have made disclosures. Using empathy therefore not only helps to establish and maintain an effective working relationship it is also integral to service-users disclosing information and to working with them effectively after such disclosures. How to develop these skills will be discussed in more depth later in this chapter.

Skills of empathic responding

In the previous chapter we explored developing the relationship with the service-user and the importance of establishing rapport. Employing such skills constitutes the beginning stage of empathic responding. Now we will take this one step further and examine the skills necessary to becoming an empathic helper.

Before we begin, consider the following activity.

ACTIVITY 3.1

Think of an example of a difficult time in your life when another person truly reached out to you by demonstrating that they were trying to understand what you were going through.

- *What effect did the helper's approach have on you?*

- *How did that leave you feeling?*

- *What did they do that was effective?*

COMMENT

It may be after considering the above question that you could be thinking there have been few times in your life when you have felt truly understood by another person.

One of the ways you can begin to be empathic with service-users is to develop and use active listening skills. The difference between listening and active listening is that with active listening you listen *and demonstrate* that you are listening. This is more difficult than it sounds. There are different ways in which you can do this.

Demonstrating that you are listening and trying to understand the service-user can take place by using skills that offer increasing levels of intensity. The most basic form of listening is where you convey understanding of the *content* of the service-user's message. Taylor (1998) states this would be where you would relay back to the service-user the content of what they have said to you in a way that they feel understood. A deeper level of engagement can be accomplished by conveying *empathic understanding* to the service-user. Here, you would try and put yourself in the service-user's shoes and attempt to work out what they might be feeling in their situation (Rogers, 1961). Empathic responding involves reading between the lines and conveying back to the service-user what they have inferred without necessarily saying outright (Miller, 2006). With this skill, you would be filling in the gaps so the person actually gains a clearer picture of what is really going on for them. We will now explore skills associated with these two areas in more depth.

Conveying understanding of content

One way of conveying understanding to the service-user is to *mirror* what they are saying. However, this technique should be used sparingly. Mirroring is repeating back exactly what the person says to highlight something of deep meaning (Clabby and O'Connor, 2004). Mirroring is useful when the speaker says something that could be construed as a 'neon light' or, in other words, something that stands out as significant, such as the following:

> Service-user: *'I feel like giving up completely.'*

You would respond with a mirroring statement:

> Social worker: *'You feel like giving up completely.'*

In this charged situation, the service-user is helped to hear exactly what they have said by metaphorically holding up a mirror to them. They then hear and engage more fully with the significance of what they are actually saying. But remember, use this technique sparingly: constantly mirroring will leave the person feeling you are just parroting, or repeating back everything they are saying and eventually their frustration will lead them to say to you 'I just said that'. Indeed, Egan (2010, p186) states that *parroting is a parody of responding with empathy*. Unfortunately, some practitioners mistake parroting for good, active listening. The key point here is that mirroring should be used very occasionally, otherwise the service-user will feel intensely frustrated with the helper.

A skill which can be used more frequently is paraphrasing. To paraphrase is to repeat back the essence of what the service-user has said using mainly your own choice of words rather than those used by the speaker (Hough, 1998). Paraphrasing helps the service-user to hear more clearly and understand better what they themselves have been saying. Nelson-Jones (2008) states that *clients' experiences may seem more real when they then hear these experiences verbalised again by their helper*. He states that good paraphrasing enables the service-user and helper to engage in a deeper understanding of what is going on for the service-user.

Examples of paraphrasing

Oprah, 40, is a service-user meeting you for the first time. She says: *I don't really know where to start. I'm not used to talking about myself.*

Helper: *It's not easy for you to begin talking to me: you are not used to sharing with others what is going on for you.*

Carlos, 25, has sought help for his drinking. He says: *All my friends are drinkers. If I want to see them it always means going to the pub and getting drunk.*

Helper: *You know that if you see your friends, alcohol will figure prominently whenever you meet up.*

Milo, 35, is having difficulty getting his 13-year-old son Ryan to school. He says: *He's up until all hours and then just won't get out of bed in the morning.*

Helper: *You are finding it very difficult to both get him to bed at a reasonable hour at night and then to get him up the following morning.*

COMMENT

The examples above focus on repeating back the essence of what the service-user has said and using such responses will encourage rapport to develop.

A point to emphasise when paraphrasing is the importance of focusing on the service-user's thinking, feelings and behaviour rather than the person they are talking about. The third example above is a case in point. It would be easy to say in the paraphrase, Ryan is staying up very late and then he refuses to get up for school in the morning. However, paraphrasing what the person who is not engaging with you is saying or doing keeps the focus on this person rather than your service-user. Always make sure your paraphrase focuses on what your service-user, i.e. the person in front of you, is thinking, feeling and doing (or not doing).

A common misconception of paraphrasing is that it is purely a skill employed by helpers so the helper can better understand the service-user in order to help them. While paraphrasing does indeed help the helper, it also assists service-users to better understand themselves. Once people understand their own feelings and motivations, they are enabled to establish what they themselves need that would help them the most (Rogers, 1961; Egan, 2010).

ACTIVITY 3.2

Paraphrasing

Try paraphrasing the following statements:

1. *The progression of my disability has been a real blow to me. I have had to stop driving now and this is having a major impact on my life.*

2. *I can't just have one or two drinks, I always have to finish the bottle of wine, and as often as not I'll open and drink a second.*

3. *I wish my sister would stop interfering and telling me what to do the whole time.*

COMMENT

Examples of paraphrasing could look something similar to the following:

1. *Your illness has hit you really hard, not least because not being able to drive is really affecting your independence.*

2. *Once you start drinking there is something inside you that compels you to drink more and more. It is as if the 'I've had enough' message never kicks in.*

3. *It sounds as if it is very difficult for you to get through to your sister that her advice is not welcome.*

Conveying empathic understanding

Good paraphrasing, together with occasional mirroring of responses, as we have seen are essential skills in building trust and rapport with service-users and helping them feel listened to and understood. Conveying deeper levels of empathy involves taking these skills and developing them further by not only paraphrasing what the service-user has said but also reflecting back what they are feeling. Nelson-Jones (2008, p56) refers to this as *emphasising the emotional content of clients' communications*. Nelson-Jones makes the point that service-users often say 'I feel' when they mean 'I think', for example they might say *'I feel that it would be best if my mother goes into residential care'*. The person is stating what they think and, as helpers, we need to identify the difference between the two. It is important that as helpers we can recognise how the service-user might be feeling because this can enable us to have a better understanding of what is going on so that the right help can be identified.

Identifying feelings in service-users

Working out how service-users feel is a challenging task for social workers to achieve. Nelson-Jones (2008, p56) suggests some ways that feelings can be identified in service-users and these include the following:

- **Observing body language**. What are the person's non-verbal messages telling you? Are you noticing downcast eyes, closed body language; are they leaning forward or leaning away from you?

- **Listening to vocal messages**. Note when the person is talking about painful situations using perhaps a monotone voice and flat expressions. This can mean they are not in touch with the full intensity of their feelings.

- **Noticing metaphors**. This means listening for common phrases and noting the accompanying feeling, for example, *'I'm on top of the world'* (meaning 'I'm feeling really alive') or *'I've got that Monday morning feeling'* (meaning 'I have a sense of dread').

Identifying feelings is not easy and can take a lifetime to perfect (Rogers, 1961). Egan (2010) writes about the importance of identifying feelings in service-users. He states that the first step to being empathic is to be able to recognise the feeling being communicated by the service-user. He refers to this skill as *perceptiveness*. We need to be able to read feelings accurately and this can only be achieved if we have a wide knowledge of feeling words ourselves. One way to develop this skill is to keep a 'feelings vocabulary' book. Here you note down one 'feeling' word and list associated words of different intensities. For example, you might write down *'scared'* and subsequently list *'worried, frightened, afraid, anxious, terrified, panic-stricken, like a rabbit in the headlights'*. Practising writing down feeling words can help you to develop your own vocabulary and recognise more easily the feelings of service-users.

ACTIVITY 3.3

Listing feeling words

Begin a vocabulary list of words that describe feelings. Next to each word, add associated words which mirror or are variations in intensity of this feeling. For example, next to 'angry', you could add annoyed, irritated, furious, outraged.

To help in getting started with this, record a television programme that involves human relationships. Serials and soaps are ideal for this exercise. Watch the programme from the beginning and when one of the characters expresses an emotion (either verbally or via their body language) press 'pause'. Now write down the feeling that you think the character is expressing. Next, list all associated words.

Identifying feelings: distinguishing between how I would feel in this situation and how the service-user feels. Putting yourself truly in the shoes of the other person.
We discussed earlier in this chapter the importance of not assuming you know what the service-user is feeling by mistaking your own feelings for his or hers. Remember empathy is being able to establish how the other person is feeling, not how you would feel in this situation.

Janette

In order to explore the above concept further, read the following example of an interaction with a service-user called Janette. She and her husband adopted a three-year-old girl called Katie six months ago and Janette is sharing her concerns.

Janette: I had no idea how challenging it was going to be for me. Katie still doesn't sleep well and I am up four or five times in the night. Her behaviour is difficult during the day too. She either clings to me obsessively or pushes me away and her mood can change in a moment. I don't know where I am and feel completely fed up with it all. It is affecting the relationship with my husband and he is saying he wishes we had never gone ahead with the adoption. He is threatening to leave us both. I have done as much as I can, there is clearly something wrong with her and I want you to take her back into care.

Ask yourself:

1. *What would be my feelings and responses if I were in Janette's situation?*

2. *Next, try and establish what are Janette's feelings and responses. In trying to work this out try the following technique: place yourself in Janette's shoes and speak as if you were her. You would use 'I' statements for this exercise and talk about your (i.e. Janette's) situation and feelings.*

3. *What are the similarities between 1 and 2?*

4. *What are the differences between 1 and 2?*

My own responses to this case scenario are listed below, but remember your work is likely to be different from this because you too are a unique individual with your own reactions to situations. There is quite likely to be a difference in what you wrote down for question 1 and question 2, i.e. how you might feel in this situation and how you might perceive Janette to be feeling. Working out the difference between your own feelings and Janette's feelings is the first step to employing an empathic response.

Responses:

1. *If I was in this situation, my response might be different from Janette's. I might feel overwhelmed by not knowing how to respond to Katie but not ready to give up on her. I might feel I had a bigger responsibility towards Katie than to my husband and I might feel angry with my husband for wanting Katie to leave the family. I would also have feelings in my role as social worker in the frame. I would want the adoption to work out and would be worried that it was going to fail and the effect this would have on Katie.*

Continued

> **COMMENT** *continued*
>
> 2. *If I was speaking as if I was Janette, my (Janette's) thinking and feelings might be along the following lines:* I am absolutely worn out with all of this and just cannot cope any longer. I had no idea it was going to be this hard and I feel so alone. I am terrified my husband will leave me and feel resentful towards Katie because I see her as the cause of the friction between us. I feel if she was no longer in the family, everything would go back to being alright.
>
> 3. *The main similarities are that I too would feel overwhelmed with the situation and disappointed in my husband's lack of commitment.*
>
> 4. *The differences are I would see that I had a big responsibility to Katie who is my daughter. I would be feeling angry with my husband for wanting to give up. Janette is more angry with Katie and blaming her for the problems in her marriage.*

Now have a look at the following case study and try the same technique again:

> **CASE STUDY**
>
> *May*
>
> *May, 38, has problems with alcohol dependency and has been coming to see you, her alcohol advisory worker, for the last few weeks. Up to now she has been doing well but she tells you that she has had a particularly bad week because her eight-year-old dog was run over in the street after she forgot to shut her gate. She then tells you that she misses him so much that she has started drinking heavily again.*
>
> *Write down the following:*
>
> 1. *My feelings if I was in this position.*
>
> 2. *What the person talking to me might be feeling or experiencing. Write this as if you were the service-user (using 'I' statements).*
>
> 3. *The similarities and differences between 1 and 2.*
>
> *Again, your response in question 1 for each of the scenarios will be unique to you. Writing as if you were Janette and May should help you to feel more engaged and understanding of what they are both feeling, even if you might be feeling something different.*
>
> *Of course if you were working with Janette and May you would not suddenly carry on the conversation as if you were them. However, trying to understand what it is like for both of them is exactly what you are trying to achieve.*

One of the keys to being able to use empathic responses is to resist trying to solve the problem for the service-user by telling them what to do. Egan (2010) states that the goal of helping is not for the helper to solve problems, but rather to help the service-user to manage them more effectively. He argues that telling the person what to do can *rob them of self-responsibility* (Egan, 2010, p185) and helpers need to be mindful of this point. It is important to stay with the service-user in the here and now. In other words, continually ask yourself, what might this person be thinking and feeling right now and convey this back to the speaker in your communication. In the next section we will look at how you can demonstrate your understanding back to the service-user.

The 'know-how' of empathy

Using empathy skills

Once you have developed a working vocabulary and can recognise how a service-user is feeling, according to Egan (2010) the next stage in being empathic is being able to demonstrate your understanding of the feeling back to them. He refers to this as the 'know-how' of empathy. Egan (2010, p186) states that *real understanding, because it passes through you, should convey some part of you*. The 'know-how' of empathy involves putting into your own words what the service-user has said and how they might be feeling. By doing this, you can make explicit what the person has *implied* from what they have told you. This constitutes empathic listening. Egan (2010, p186) writes,

> To avoid parroting, tap into the processing you've been doing as you listened, come at what the client has said from a slightly different angle, use your own words, change the order, refer to an expressed but unnamed emotion – let the client-in-context flow through you and then do whatever you can to let the client know that you are working at understanding.

In other words, think about what the service-user is telling you, identify their feelings, then put this into your own words and say this back to the person.

In the example of working with Janette above we have already tried to put ourselves in her shoes by using the technique of speaking as if we were Janette. Of course you would not speak to Janette like this, rather you would then turn your 'I' statements into 'you' statements and speak directly to Janette. An empathic statement might look like this:

> I can see how difficult this has been for you over the last six months. You are absolutely exhausted because you are hardly getting any sleep and feeling worn down with all the responsibility. I can also see that you are feeling unsupported with the challenge of caring for Katie and despairing that the situation will not get any better. It must be very difficult because you are feeling you only have two choices: saving your relationship or continuing to care for Katie.

This is likely to be different from how you as a helper might feel and by working through it this way demonstrates that you have remained focused on Janette. Remember, at this stage in the helping process you are focusing on Janette's feelings. Try not to be tempted to move into a problem-solving mode too early: telling her what to do will alienate your service-user because she will feel that you are not listening to her. At a later stage, when feelings have been explored more fully, you will move into assisting Janette to explore what might help her to develop some supportive strategies. These skills will be explored in later chapters of this book.

Using 'you feel... because...'

According to Egan (2010, p167) a way of developing your practice of empathic responses is to use the formula *'You are feeling... because...'* Using this formula shows that you are attempting to understand what the service-user is really saying and feeling. It will help to build the trust between you both and enable the person to recognise what is happening to them more clearly. It would also demonstrate empathy. This can appear a little harsh when you see it in print like this. At first glance it seems direct and implies you have to get it right first time. However, Rogers (1961, p53), in discussing attempts at empathy makes the following comment:

> *I am often impressed with the fact that even a minimal amount of empathic understanding – a bumbling and faulty attempt to catch the confused complexity of the client's meaning – is helpful.*

In other words, try to state what you think a service-user might be feeling back to them because it is your *attempt* at empathy that is important in developing the relationship. If you get it wrong, it is not so bad: the service-user will soon put you right and the relationship will be strengthened because you tried.

Rogers (1961, p53) goes on to ask:

> *Can I step into the client's private world and sense it so accurately that I can catch not only the meanings of his experience which are obvious to him, but those meanings which are only implicit, which he sees only dimly or as confusion?*

In other words, can I help the service-user to bring into awareness that which is just out of sight to them? In the following example, Carol is seeking help with her 15-year-old son, Steven. She says:

> *When he gets into one of those moods I just can't seem to do anything with him. I have to be careful not to say the wrong thing because, well... I would rather not say.*

A statement that re-phrases Carol's words would be:

> *When he gets into a bad mood you have to be careful not to say anything that might upset him. You would rather not go into details.*

As we have stated already, merely re-phrasing what the service-user has told you may demonstrate that you have heard what she has said on the surface but it does not necessarily demonstrate that you have engaged with what she is really saying underneath.

ACTIVITY 3.4

Imagine you are working with Carol, what do you think she is really saying to you? What is she hinting at or implying? Write down your response using the formula 'You feel... because...'.

COMMENT

Although she has not used the word 'anxious', Carol has certainly expressed this emotion. In saying she would rather not say any more, she is stating that she feels worried about not being in control of the situation.

Therefore, an empathic response back to Carol could consist of the following:

It sounds as if when Steven becomes angry you feel afraid of him and anxious because you have lost control of the situation.

This response would help Carol to recognise better her own feelings and responses and to bring into awareness that which is just outside of conscious awareness, i.e. her fear of the consequences of not being able to control her son. It also gives her a chance, if necessary, to correct you. She might say to you in response, No, it's not that. I feel I would leave the house and keep running, never coming back.

As we can see from the above, using empathic responses is a way of developing deeper understanding of the service-user and, more to the point, also helping service-users to gain deeper understanding of themselves.

Imagining your supervisor asks you what you think is really going on for the service-user

One of the ways to work out what the person you are working with might be thinking or feeling is to imagine that your supervisor asks you *'What do you think is going on for your service-user at the moment? What is she thinking and feeling?'* In that moment when we engage with the questioner and let our guard down, we can really get in touch with what might be happening for the person.

In order to illustrate this technique, imagine you are working with Marilyn as her family adoption social worker. She says to you:

I have always wanted children and when I found out I couldn't have any, once I had come to terms with this, I thought about adoption as a positive way forward. I would feel privileged to be considered for this.

Now let us have a look at how we can attempt an empathic response to Marilyn. Remember Rogers (1961) talks about how difficult this is to accomplish well and how rare it is for a listener to engage in a deep level of understanding with a service-user. Nevertheless, we will make an attempt.

ACTIVITY 3.5

Re-read Marilyn's statement, then, imagine your supervisor has been a fly on the wall. She asks you, What do you think Marilyn is really implying here? What do you think she has gone through to get to the place she is now?

Write down what your thoughts are about Marilyn's situation and her feelings and what you would say to your supervisor.

COMMENT

My thoughts about Marilyn and what I would say to my supervisor about her are the following: I think she has been through a great deal of heartache in the past. She has clearly had a great desire to have children. It has been painful for her to discover she cannot give birth herself. She may have experienced considerable feelings of loss and she may have felt she would never be able to become a mother. This has taken some time to accept. She has thought hard about what future she wants for herself and this involves having children in her life by adopting if she is accepted, although she does not see adoption as an automatic right.

The next step is to make the shift from thinking about your response in the third person (Marilyn is...she feels...) to how you would say this as an empathic reflection back to Marilyn. My response might be along the following lines:

> It sounds as if you have been through a great deal of heartache in the past because of your infertility. I can see how much you have wanted to have children and it must have been so painful to find out that you could not give birth. You have given yourself time to adjust to this news and are now ready to look at what would be involved in adopting a child.

It can be seen from this technique that in the moment when we imagine someone else asking us what is going on for the service-user we can gain a deeper sense of their feelings.

ACTIVITY 3.6

Try putting into practice all the skills you have developed so far. Read the following example of an interaction with Bernard and imagine he is talking to you about the possibility of going into residential care. Remember we discussed the difference between a service-user's organismic self (their true self) and their self-concept (how others want them to be) earlier in the chapter. Bear this in mind when you are thinking about what you might say to Bernard.

Bernard says to you, his social worker:

> I've been well looked after in the hospital since my accident and I know that I will be leaving here soon. My daughter thinks I ought to go into a home because she is worried I won't be able to cope on my own. She has been very good to me and I don't want to be a burden to her so perhaps I ought to do as she suggests.

What do you think Bernard is really saying to you? Write this down first using 'he'. Then write down what you would actually say, as an empathic response, to Bernard.

COMMENT

Remember that at this stage you are not looking for a solution, you are trying to focus on what Bernard is telling you and trying to understand what it is like for him. In other words, you are empathising with him.

Remember that practising skills is the key to becoming an empathic practitioner, so make sure you use any opportunity presented to you to develop this way of engaging.

ACTIVITY 3.7

It would be useful to return to the recording you made of a television serial or soap (suggested earlier in this chapter). You have already written down what you think your chosen character is feeling. Now write down what you would say to the character if you were their social worker.

Using assertiveness in empathic responding

Assertiveness is explored more fully in Chapter 5 but it is also important to include this way of working in our exploration of empathic responding. Egan (2010) states that in offering verbal empathic responses to the service-user, we might also need to use assertiveness. What he means here is having the courage to be congruent (which means being open and honest) with the person and to say with care and respect how we might see their situation. This might include expressing our hunches of how they might be feeling about us. In social work this is an essential skill because it helps us to remain truthful and transparent and enables the service-user to be honest with us. With this in mind, read and work through the following activity.

ACTIVITY 3.8

Maeve is 88 and has recently gone to live in residential care permanently, having experienced multiple health problems. You talked with her extensively before her move and were careful to make sure you established what her wishes and feelings were. She now says she is not sure any more. She misses her neighbours, her flat and her old life. She says she thinks the move has been a mistake.

Write down what you would say to Maeve as an empathic response.

COMMENT

Maeve might be feeling that you are in part to blame for her move into residential care. A good, assertive empathic response will acknowledge this and state it openly. For example, you could say:

Maeve, you have been through a really big upheaval because of moving from your flat into residential care. I can see how much you are missing all the things you have lost

Continued

COMMENT *continued*

such as daily contact with people you know and the belongings you had to sell from your flat. You are feeling upset because it has all been such a massive change from everything you have known for all those years. I know we talked a great deal about this move and I wonder if you are feeling a little angry towards me too because of my part in this.

In this example, by the helper asserting how the service-user may be feeling angry with them, the service-user is enabled to explore more fully how they feel towards the helper. This can deepen the relationship and help the person to experience more fully their organismic self (who they really are).

We will now move on to exploring all three of these skills in combination: identifying feelings, using the know-how of empathy and assertiveness.

Bringing skills together: Identifying feelings, using know-how and assertiveness

To summarise Egan's theory (2010), first we have to identify how the service-user might be feeling. Then we employ skills in empathic responding, using assertiveness when necessary. In the final case example of this chapter, all three of these skills are applied.

CASE STUDY

Ryan

Let us return to Ryan, the 13-year-old young person who is not getting up in time to go to school. Imagine you are his social worker and having your first session with Ryan. He is sitting in front of you with his arms and legs crossed and saying he hates school and can find more interesting things to do at home. He is looking at the floor and will not give you eye contact. Let us work through Egan's pointers:

Identifying feelings

I might perceive that Ryan is feeling uncomfortable, embarrassed, annoyed with me for being in his home, angry that a professional outsider is now involved, defiant and cornered. He might also be feeling worried that he has been caught not attending school.

Using know-how and assertiveness

Having identified some possible feelings, I would frame these into a sentence or two to convey to Ryan that I am trying to put myself into his shoes and work out what is going on for him. Until I do this, I will have little chance of forming a working alliance with him. I choose to say the following:

Ryan, I can see how hard this is for you. My sense is that you are feeling pretty uncomfortable both about me being here in your home and also because we both know you have not been going to school. If I were in your shoes I would be feeling somewhat cornered right now. I want to work with you to find out why going to school is difficult for you.

COMMENT

In the above example, the social worker has to be mindful of creating and developing a working relationship with Ryan. Koprowska (2010) states that a good social work relationship involves warmth, respect and friendliness and these conditions underpin an empathic approach. Listening to Ryan and observing his non-verbal communication helps to develop perceptiveness (Egan, 2010) of how Ryan might be feeling. Trying to sit in Ryan's shoes will assist in identifying his feelings, and recognise that this might be different from how we might be feeling in this situation. Once we have established how Ryan might be feeling, we then convey our understanding using a respectful and tentative approach using 'I' statements and self-disclosure. Saying 'If I were in your shoes I would be feeling somewhat cornered right now' *can help Ryan to feel understood and more likely to engage. As social workers we also need to deliver a respectful but clear and assertive message which establishes our role and how we can help. Saying* 'I want to work with you to find out why going to school is difficult for you' *states clearly that our aim is to work with Ryan to find out why he is avoiding school and to develop strategies for helping him to return.*

Using empathic responding skills and trying to see the world through the service-user's eyes can help them to feel the social worker is genuinely interested. If service-users feel understood then they are more likely to engage with the social worker in finding solutions to difficulties.

CHAPTER SUMMARY

In this chapter, we have defined empathy and established why it is an important social work skill. We have discussed how to convey understanding back to the service-user and the difference between mirroring, parroting, paraphrasing and empathic responding. The stages in empathic responding have been described: we have explored how the first stage involves identifying service-users' feelings and distinguishing between how the person might feel and how the social worker may feel in the same situation. We have looked at the importance of using the right words in conveying accurate understanding of feelings to service-users and the role of a 'feelings vocabulary' in developing this skill. We have then explored the 'know-how' of empathy by developing a range of different techniques such as 'you feel… because…' and imagining a supervisor is asking us to explain what is going on for the service-user. Finally, we have explored the importance of using assertiveness skills in empathic responding to help the service-user to understand our role as the social worker and to assist in working through conflict. Assertiveness and challenging skills will be explored more thoroughly in later chapters.

If you have read this chapter carefully, worked through the exercises and reflection points, and engaged in the wider reading suggested below you will have come to the realisation that empathic responding is a very difficult skill to accomplish well. From my experience of teaching counselling skills both to counselling students and social workers in training, the most able students are those who recognise that being skilled in empathic responding is a constant challenge requiring endless practise. I remember once facilitating a skills class where one student said, when hearing the aim of the session was to develop empathy skills, *'but Sally, we did empathy last week'*. If you now have a wry smile on your face in response to this statement, you are several steps along the way towards becoming an empathic practitioner.

FURTHER READING

Egan, G (2010) *The skilled helper: A problem management and opportunity development approach to helping*. 9th edition. Belmont, CA: Brooks/Cole.

Chapter 6, Empathic responding: working at mutual understanding, pp161–87 explores in depth the perceptiveness, know-how and assertiveness of empathic responding.

Lindsay, T (2009) *Social work intervention*. Exeter: Learning Matters.

Chapter 2, Person-centred approaches, pp20–35 offers a good overview of person-centred theory.

Rogers, C (1961) *On becoming a person: A therapist's view of psychotherapy*. London: Constable.

All of Rogers' text is helpful to gaining an understanding of empathic responding. However, Chapter 3, The characteristics of a helping relationship, pp39–58 is particularly relevant.

Chapter 4

Overcoming barriers

Introduction

According to the Oxford English Dictionary (2009) a barrier is something that gets in the way, something *that bars advance or prevents access*. It is very important that as practitioners we are able to recognise barriers as they are highly significant in communication. We need to understand how barriers are created in the engagement process with each individual service-user. It is also essential that we find ways of overcoming barriers if we are to create meaningful and successful working relationships. Sometimes in our interactions we might feel that what appears to be happening on the surface is not necessarily what is really happening underneath. We may become aware that there are unconscious processes occurring in the relationship between ourselves and the service-user that are having a detrimental effect on the outcome. A key aspect of this chapter is to define and focus on the unconscious barriers that occur in the helping relationship. We will do this by exploring concepts such as transference, counter-transference and Transactional Analysis, all of which can help us to work out what might really be happening between ourselves and the service-user. There will also be a focus on self-development exercises to enable us to develop awareness of, and overcome, our own barriers.

What are barriers?

Barriers stop the helping relationship from working effectively. As practitioners we need to focus on what we might consciously, or more subtly unconsciously, do which may deter the service-user from wanting to engage with us. Moss (2008, p41) describes barriers as

> *...any action, behaviour or physical arrangement that discourages the other person from feeling comfortable, thereby reducing their ability to communicate positively and effectively.*

The skills explored in previous chapters will have given you an indication of how easy it is to put up barriers. For example, we have already described how if we 'parrot' the speaker, rather than paraphrase their nuances and implied meaning, then this will quickly leave the person thinking 'but I just said that'.

Barriers can be categorised into three areas: level one barriers, which can be quite easily identified; level two barriers, which are less obvious; and level three barriers, which are often unconscious and the most difficult to identify and work with. Thus, barriers range from those easily recognised to those which are difficult to spot and which require a higher level of self-knowledge before they can be identified. This chapter acknowledges the barriers which are easy to identify but will focus more fully on our unconscious barriers, i.e. those which are more difficult to identify.

Level one barriers

These barriers are quite simple to identify and can be easily eliminated with a little fore-thought. The following activities are examples of impediments to effective engagement. With a little thinking beforehand, you can take steps to avoid or overcome these barriers.

- Having a desk between you and the service-user. This leaves you in a position of authority. If the desk cannot be moved, sit beside the other person.

- Continually or surreptitiously checking your watch.

- Answering your mobile phone during interactions.

- Fiddling with your hair or playing with your pen.

- Closed body language (such as crossing your legs away from the speaker).

- Failure on your part to engage a translator when the service-user does not speak English.

- Focusing on writing notes rather than demonstrating that you are listening to the speaker.

ACTIVITY 4.1

Think of a situation where you engaged with someone who wanted to talk to you about a problem. What level one barriers did you put up? How might these have affected your engagement? What could you have changed to limit the impact of each barrier?

> **COMMENT**
>
> *Think about the physical barriers in the room, such as desks or tables. Perhaps your conversation took place on the phone and you were not able to witness the other person's physical reaction to you. If you are not sure how you present yourself non-verbally, set up a trio and ask an observer to give you constructive feedback on this aspect of your communication.*

Level two barriers

Level two barriers are those which may lead into difficulties before you realise what is happening. They arise when we fail to use theory and lessons about good practice to underpin our communication and engagement skills. They also occur when we concentrate more on our own issues and problems rather than those brought by the service-user. Examples include:

- letting your mind wander on to other thoughts when the service-user is talking to you so you realise you do not know what they have just said;

- when the service-user talks to you about an event that reminds you of something you have found difficult in your own life and you begin to think about this instead of listening;

- taking over the conversation and talking about yourself rather than encouraging service-users to talk about themselves;

- asking one question after another so the service-user feels bombarded and eventually sits there waiting for you to lead the session further;

- jumping in because there is a silence: this can interrupt valuable thinking time for the service-user;

- failing to give eye contact, leaving the service-user experiencing you as disinterested;

- focusing too much on your response to the other person and consequently not hearing something they have said;

- giving advice from the stance of what you would do in the same situation rather than helping the service-user devise their own way forward.

Level two barriers can be eliminated by developing more awareness of how the service-user experiences us and by using theory to underpin our skills. These barriers all contribute to the service-user ceasing to engage with us on anything other than a superficial level. Being more in touch with what is going on for us in the present moment would help to eliminate these areas.

ACTIVITY **4.2**

Return to the conversation you considered in activity 4.1. Can you identify any level two barriers of which you have now become aware? How might these barriers have affected your engagement? What do you need to do to eliminate these barriers in future?

COMMENT

It is easy for all of us to deploy the level one and level two barriers described above. The key to not falling into these traps is to use the helping skills we have already developed and to constantly monitor our own practice. The next set of barriers are the most difficult to overcome.

Level three barriers

These barriers are those we put up unconsciously and, as such, they are much harder to identify and change. They arise from using our ingrained and familiar patterns of behaviour which we learned in our own childhood and which we repeat without awareness in our adult interactions. In exploring level three barriers, this section will draw from Freud (1916), Casement (1985) and Jacobs (2005) to define unconscious processes, transference and counter-transference and explore how each of these can act as barriers to working effectively with service-users.

Unconscious processes

In psychodynamic theory, Freud (1916) defines *the unconscious* as that which is concealed or inaccessible to us and which consists of often uncomfortable feelings from early childhood events which we then repeat in our adult interactions. For example, a service-user might remind us of a significant person from our own childhood and we may unconsciously respond to them in a similar way. Jacobs (2010) writes that we often do not make these connections until someone else points them out to us. The obvious place for this to happen is within supervision where we can both draw on our supervisor's extensive experience and obtain feedback on our own interactions (Jacobs, 2005; Casement, 1985). Both the practitioner and the service-user can be heavily influenced by unconscious processes, which can then create barriers to meaningful communication. These types of barriers then, arise from our own and our service-users' learned and deep-seated patterns of thought, feelings and behaviour.

We often engage with other people in the way we are most comfortable with ourselves. However, our service-user is likely to be different from us and the way we might deal with something may not be the same for them. If we fail to develop awareness of such differences then these will become barriers. For example, our sense of humour might be different from that of the service-user and if we are not careful, we could offend them.

One example of a level three barrier involves something known as *transference* and this will be described next.

Transference

The term *transference* describes how we unconsciously use our past experiences to shape how we think, feel and act in current situations. Early childhood relationships strongly influence how people act as adults and we *transfer* emotional responses from childhood into our adult relationships (Hough, 1998 and 2001). The trigger for transference can be initiated by either the service-user or the practitioner and involves one party engaging in a manner which echoes some aspect of the other person's past (Casement, 1985).

An example of transference is illustrated in the following case study.

CASE STUDY

Helen is a social worker in the Leaving Care Team and for the past 12 months has been working with Mark, 17, to prepare him for living independently. Mark first came into care when he was five years old because of his parents' dependence on drugs and their inability to look after him. He has had several foster care placements, all of which have broken down and he has lived in a local authority children's home since he was 14. Last week, Helen had to miss her appointment with Mark because her mother suddenly became ill and she took a few days off work to look after her. Helen telephoned Mark to postpone the meeting with him to this week. She thought she had developed a good relationship with Mark and so was surprised when he was sullen and uncommunicative with her in the rescheduled appointment. When Helen asked him how he was, he replied why would you care? Afterwards, Helen's supervisor helps her to see that Mark's experience is that a number of key people have given up on him in his life, beginning with both his parents. When Helen was unable to meet with Mark she became another person in a long list whom he feels has withdrawn from him. Mark is reminded of past feelings of loss and the associated pain. He has transferred his earlier feelings of abandonment onto Helen and is likely to keep repeating this with other people to whom he gets close.

Other forms of transference include when the service-user responds to you, the practitioner, automatically in the same way as they have done to significant others in their lives. Jacobs (2010) describes this as where the service-user is reacting to you *as if* you were, say, their parent. A service-user who has experienced a dominant and directive parent may *transfer* this expectation to you and insist you tell them what to do. They repeat the expectations they have of their parent. This then becomes a barrier in the helping process because, if you respond by being directive, the service-user is likely to become dependent upon you to tell them what to do. In consequence, service-users do not develop the ability to take responsibility for themselves and fail to become autonomous decision makers in their own right. Your response to the service-user is important and this will be explored in the next section.

ACTIVITY 4.3

Samantha, 30, is a practitioner working with Betty who is 60 and whose husband is in the later stages of a terminal illness. Betty has a daughter, Meg, who is the same age as Samantha and towards whom she is very protective. She has not shared with her daughter how sad she feels about her husband's impending death because she feels this would really upset Meg. Samantha previously cared for someone in her family who died and considers sharing this information with Betty, believing this will help her to feel more understood.

* *What might be the effect of Samantha sharing this information with Betty?*

* *How might this be explained in terms of transference?*

COMMENT

Betty is likely to feel similarly protective towards Samantha because, being 30, Samantha may remind her of Meg. In the same way she does not want to upset Meg, she may not want to upset Samantha. Betty may therefore transfer the protective feelings she has for Meg onto Samantha. Consequently, any disclosure Samantha makes about her own loss may become a barrier to Betty being able to share her feelings of loss with Samantha.

Counter-transference

When transference occurs, the response evoked in the other person in the transaction is known as counter-transference. One example of counter-transference is the process of feelings that are evoked in the practitioner by the service-user (Jacobs, 2010). If, in response to something the service-user has divulged, the social worker transfers feelings from their own past into the current interaction with the other person, counter-transference is said to have taken place. To illustrate this, let us explore further the earlier case study by looking at Helen's counter-transference.

CASE STUDY

Helen, Mark's social worker, feels guilty and that she has seriously failed him when she postponed the meeting. Helen's background is different from Mark's. She is an only child, brought up within her birth family and had a happy childhood until her father left home for another woman when Helen was eight years old. For a long time her mother was devastated by this event. Helen submerged her own feelings of loss, feeling any such display would upset her mother further. She tried to look after her mother by pleasing her as much as possible and by doing everything she could not to upset her. In supervision, Helen's supervisor helps Helen to see that when Mark says to her 'why would you care?', strong feelings from her own childhood are evoked. Her unconscious memories of not wanting to upset her mother lead her to replicate this event and so feel guilty that she is responsible for upsetting Mark. This is Helen's counter-transference. If Helen remains unaware of this unconscious process, she is likely to be over-apologetic to Mark. Doing this keeps Mark from exploring his own over-reaction to Helen's (and other

Continued

---

people's) absences. If Helen can become consciously aware of what underpins her own strong reaction, it will cease to become a barrier to her, thereby helping Mark to explore his underlying feelings and subsequent behaviour. If she can identify how she feels in response to Mark's sentiments, Helen can help him to explore this too:

Mark: *Why would you care?*

Helen (instead of apologising): *I know you feel let down by my not being here last week. You have shown me a really strong, angry reaction to this and I'm wondering if it might be useful for us to explore this and where it comes from a little more.*

Let us explore counter-transference further in the following case study.

CASE STUDY

William received lots of messages from his parents in his early life that 'big boys don't cry'. Now, as an adult, when he is upset, William tries to avoid thinking about what he is sad about by doing something else. This usually involves him going for a run or distracting himself by watching a film. William is a foster carer and has recently begun looking after a ten-year-old boy called Kevin. Kevin is very upset about being separated from his mother who is too ill to look after him and cries about this in William's company. Because crying has not been allowed for William during his own childhood, he feels uncomfortable when Kevin cries and his first thought is I must stop Kevin from crying, I'll try and make him think about something else. *Instead of being empathic with Kevin while he is upset (by reflecting back Kevin's feelings of sadness), William says,* Oh Kevin, don't cry. Look, Dr Who is going to be on the television soon, it's your favourite programme isn't it? *William interacts with Kevin in the same way he would deal with himself, i.e. by using distraction. William withdraws from Kevin by putting up a barrier, which sends the message that any engagement involving the expression of sadness is disallowed. William is repeating his own pattern of behaviour and imposing this on Kevin without any awareness of what he is doing and the effect it is having.*

In this case study we see how William's counter-transference response to tears mirrors the way he has learned to manage his own sadness. William deflects his own sadness by watching films. Similarly, he distracts Kevin away from tears by turning on the television.

The examples above demonstrate that counter-transference reactions often belong to earlier periods in the helper's life and may have little to do with service-users themselves (Jacobs, 2010). Further examples of counter-transference include the following:

- You are working with Neville, a male service-user you dislike but cannot quite put your finger on why this is the case. Your feelings are leading you to act in a defensive way. He has a habit of tapping his fingers on the table when he is listening to you and, eventually, you realise that your aunt does exactly the same thing when she is about to criticise you. Although the service-user has never become angry with you, you associate the trait of finger tapping as an indication of a forthcoming verbal attack. Until you make the connection, you are likely to carry on acting defensively with Neville. Once you make the connection and recognise that Neville is different from your aunt, this barrier of counter-transference can be overcome.

- You are making various assumptions about some of your service-users that are based on your own values and belief systems. For example, you are working with 75-year-old Wilf who is talking to you about his desire to move to the coast. Your (stereotypical) belief is that older people are incapable of change and because of this you *transfer* your beliefs onto Wilf by advising him to stay where he is. You do not recognise how your own belief system fails to place Wilf as the decision maker in his own life.

At other times, feelings and responses evoked in the practitioner can be directly related to the attitude and behaviour of the service-user rather than arising from the practitioner's own past. For example, Adrian is a service-user who talks over you, interrupts and always seems to dismiss anything you have to say as unimportant. When he says he is afraid his wife is going to leave him but has no idea why, you speculate that his wife feels as over-whelmed by his interpersonal style as you do. Being in touch with your reaction can be a starting point in helping him to overcome this blind spot he has about himself. The coun-ter-transference in this instance is not a barrier; rather it is an enabler to a deeper level of understanding. Sharing your experience of Adrian with him is referred to as being congru-ent, i.e. honest and open about how you perceive him (Rogers, 1961). Helping Adrian to see himself as others see him can help him to work on his own difficulties.

ACTIVITY 4.4

Think of a situation when you have felt a strong reaction during an interaction with someone else. Ask yourself the following questions:

- *How did you react to the person?*
- *Was your reaction related exclusively to the other person?*
- *Did the service-user have a particular trait or way of being that reminded you of a feeling you have experienced with someone else at an earlier stage in your life?*
- *If you answered yes to the previous question, at what point did you become aware of this?*
- *Knowing what you know now, how could you have responded differently to the person with whom you were interacting?*

COMMENT

If the person reminded you of or displayed a trait similar to someone from your past and you did not realise this at the time, it is likely that you became caught up in an uncom-fortable interaction which left you feeling uneasy and out of control. Learning about how and why we react in certain ways can help us to identify why our responses sometimes can become barriers to a deeper level of engagement.

If we can begin to recognise the unconscious processes which are taking place between ourselves and our service-users then this can go a long way to overcoming barriers. The examples discussed above are the tip of the iceberg when it comes to identifying level three barriers and it is likely that you will uncover all kinds of traits and behaviours which will get in the way of engaging at a deeper level. A good supervisor can help practitioners to recognise transference and counter-transference by exploring what was said, the likely mutual effects and how the responses have been influenced. Indeed, Hawkins and Shohet (2007) comment that by engaging in this process, the supervisor can help the practitioner to see, for example, how the service-user unconsciously conveys their real needs to the helper. Identifying the service-user's deeper needs then, helps to prevent barriers in understanding from occurring.

If you are open to receiving feedback about transference and counter-transference, you will be well on the way to becoming a more skilled practitioner. However, trying to work out how such unconscious processes affect our interactions is not easy. One theory which can help us to become more aware of this important area is Transactional Analysis and in the next section we will explore this way of working.

Transactional Analysis

Transactional Analysis is a theory based on how people interact with one another. The theory was devised by Eric Berne (1971) and is influenced by Freudian concepts in that Berne believed that our early experiences influence how we interact with one another.

Having an understanding of Transactional Analysis can help us to recognise where our communication style is both helpful and a barrier to engaging on a deeper level with service-users. The theory enables us to analyse the words and phrases we use and to choose different responses when our communication style becomes a barrier.

An important aspect of Transactional Analysis is the study of *ego-states,* which are *coherent systems of thought and feeling manifested by corresponding patterns of behaviour* (Berne, 1975, p11). According to Berne, the ego-states contain all of our unconscious ways of relating. He describes us as having three ego-states: the Parent; the Adult; and the Child. The following diagram (Figure 4.1) illustrates thinking, feeling and behaviour related to the ego-states and this is followed by a more detailed explanation below.

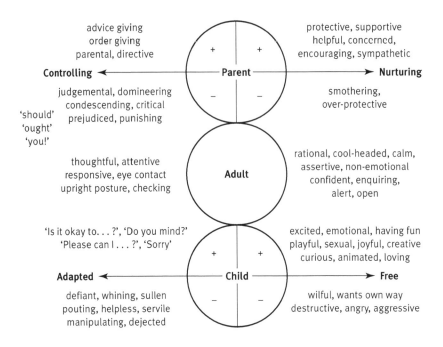

Figure 4.1 Ego-states (Hewson, 1990)

RESEARCH SUMMARY

The Parent ego-state

The Parent ego-state consists of thinking, feelings and behaviour which we copied from our parents or parental figures when we were young (Berne, 1975; Stewart and Joines, 1987). Berne states we then repeat these patterns as adults. Our Parent ego-state is divided into two halves. The first half is called the Controlling Parent and when we engage with this ego-state our behaviour manifests as being critical and controlling, giving orders and making judgements. There are two sides to our Controlling Parent: positive and negative (Stewart and Joines, 1987). We could be said to be in our positive Controlling Parent when we are being controlling for good reasons. For example, if a child under our supervision begins to run out into the road, we might grab them and say loudly, don't do that, there's a car coming! In this situation, it is appropriate and necessary that we take control quickly and forcefully otherwise an accident may occur. Other examples of positive controlling messages we may remember from childhood are eat your greens, they are good for you...you must be in bed by 9.00pm...don't go outside without putting on a warm coat. As an adult, we remember these messages and can repeat similar ones. An example of being in our positive Controlling Parent as an adult might be when we take control in an emergency situation. If a person at work collapses on the floor we could direct a colleague to place them in the recovery position while telling another to call an ambulance. This is entirely appropriate action in the circumstances. However, we can be said to be in our negative Controlling Parent when we take control or tell someone what to do when they are quite capable of making decisions for themselves.

Continued

Examples of how we operate in our negative Controlling Parent ego-state include when we are critical, condescending, prejudiced, dictatorial and use statements such as you should…, you shouldn't…., you ought to…, you are a bad person, you are stupid…, don't… etc. Stewart and Joines (1987) describe the negative Controlling Parent as containing a put-down in one way or another. Our body language can also portray our negative Controlling Parent ego-state where we are likely to tap our fingers and/or feet, fold our arms, frown and invade the other person's space. The message from our behaviour is one of I know better than you *and what is more,* I am better than you. *This, of course, is the opposite of all we have previously defined as effective counselling and communication skills in social work. Talking to service-users using our negative Controlling Parent will place a major barrier between us and encourage a Child reaction in return. This will be explored later in the chapter.*

The other aspect of our Parent ego-state is made up of the Nurturing Parent. *Here, we replay behaviours which our parents and caregivers displayed to us when we were little and in need (Stewart and Joines, 1987). Examples here include when we look after or comfort someone. Again, the Nurturing Parent is divided into positive and negative sides. If you were saying to an older service-user in residential care* let me know if you would like some help getting dressed *then this would be offering genuine support for the person and acting from your positive Nurturing Parent ego-state. You would also be enabling them to accept or refuse the offer of help. If, however, you went into the person's room and said* let's get you dressed, *without checking whether or not the person was able to do this for themselves, then this would be an example of being in your negative Nurturing Parent ego-state. In other words, you would be taking over and consequently smothering the person.*

A good question to ask ourselves when deciding whether we are in our positive or negative Nurturing Parent is for us to ask ourselves the following question: am I doing something for this person that they are able to do for themselves? *If the answer is yes, then the negative side of this ego-state is in operation and we need to change our approach. Again, taking over and acting in our negative Nurturing Parent creates barriers by not enabling the service-user to develop autonomy for their own decisions and actions.*

The Child ego-state

The Child ego-state contains behaviour which we learned in childhood from our own caregivers and which we now repeat in adulthood (Berne, 1971). As adults, we often replay traits from when we were young. These can include being nice, stubborn, happy, sad, naughty, flexible, spontaneous and fitting in with others' needs. The Child ego-state is divided into two halves. One half is called the Adapted Child *and the other half is called the* Free Child.

How we behave in our Adapted Child depends on patterns of behaviour we learned in our own childhood. It is the side of us which adapts to others' desires and expectations and what we do to win approval or to get attention (Stewart and Joines, 1987).

Continued

The Adapted Child ego-state is again divided into positive and negative. In my positive Adapted Child I might deliberately do something to please someone else in order to gain their approval. For example, as a child I might have learned that finishing all the food on my plate pleased my parent who had cooked the meal. As an adult, visiting a friend who cooks a meal for me, I could be said to be in my Adapted Child ego-state if I eat everything on the plate when I do not like the food or am full.

An example of behaviour from our negative Adapted Child ego-state is when we might sulk in response to not having our needs met or become silent, whining, sullen or rebellious instead of expressing how we feel. As an adult working in social care I would have to be careful not to slip into familiar Adapted Child patterns of behaviour of wanting to please the service-user. An example might be when the service-user wants a particular service and because you want to please them, you promise to provide this before checking whether or not the service is available.

We are said to be in our positive Free Child when we re-create being spontaneous, having fun, feeling happy or sad, being playful, creative, curious and funny. Our negative Free Child manifests when we are being naughty, wilful, stubborn, demanding and selfish. For example, if, as a child I learned that having a tantrum resulted in getting my own way, as an adult I am likely to repeat this behaviour from my Free Child and get angry, shout and loudly protest when I want something, hoping that the other person will capitulate.

The Adult ego-state

Operating from the Parent and Child ego-states involves unconscious responses to situations from our past. In our Child ego-state, we replay material from our own past and in our Parent ego-state, we borrow material from our parental figures (Stewart, 1989). In the Adult ego-state, which is the third and final ego-state, we act in ways which are direct and appropriate responses to what is going on in the here and now as opposed to replaying behaviour, thoughts and feelings from our childhood and our parental figures (Stewart, 1989). Because of this, the Adult is not divided into any other sections.

The Adult ego-state consists of behaviour which is rational, assertive, calm and logical (Berne, 1971). It also consists of feelings which enable us to manage problems as well as thinking-type behaviour. For example, if I find myself in a setting where someone is physically threatening me it is natural that I will feel scared. This is an Adult reaction to a dangerous situation and one which motivates me to leave quickly.

Operating in our Adult ego-state involves us using full conscious awareness to assess how we are acting, reacting and communicating with the service-user. Examples include when we are in touch with what we are thinking and feeling and are able to convey this to the service-user in a calm, clear and direct manner.

ACTIVITY 4.5

Think of a recent stressful interaction you had with someone which ended with you feeling bad or uncomfortable. Write down what happened, what your thinking, feelings and behaviour were.

- *What messages encouraged in you as a child by your parent or caregivers did you replay in the interaction?*

- *Can you identify any current feelings, thinking or behaviour which remind you of similar feelings from your childhood?*

- *What could you have done differently which would have constituted a more appropriate reaction to what was happening in the here and now with the other person?*

COMMENT

If you reacted unconsciously, it is likely that you now recognise thoughts, feelings and behaviours which are familiar to you from both your childhood and the parental messages you received. For example, if you became involved in an argument with someone in authority who shouted at you, it is likely that your reaction to this person was similar to the way you would have reacted to a parent figure when you were a child. You might therefore have responded from your Child ego-state. If you were the one who was becoming angry, upset or annoyed with someone else, your behaviour could have consisted of traits that you have unconsciously copied from your parents or caregivers. You may have then given a Parent ego-state response. Thinking about what you could have done differently and considering giving a different reaction from the one you might have given without thinking first are initial steps in accessing your Adult ego-state. In the next section, we will explore this further.

Analysing transactions

Developing our understanding of which ego state we are using, together with the effect this can have on the service-user, is very useful in helping us to analyse the effectiveness of our communication. Berne (1971) states that once we become aware of our own ego-states and how as individuals we think, feel and behave we can choose to change our responses. Changing our ego-state can then invite the other person to change theirs.

Let us explore this in more detail by applying these concepts to Andy, a social worker who is working with Zenda. Andy is helping Zenda to develop her parenting skills with her two young children whom she is finding difficult to control. In last week's session, Andy helped Zenda to work out strategies to get the children to bed on time each night. During the session, Andy asks how things are going and Zenda confesses she has not been at all successful with this task. Because she is quite frightened that Andy has the power to take her children away, she finds it difficult to be honest and tell Andy where and how she is struggling. Pleasing Andy therefore becomes a priority for Zenda. When Zenda tells Andy she has not been able to get the children to bed on time, Andy frowns, sighs and the following transaction takes place:

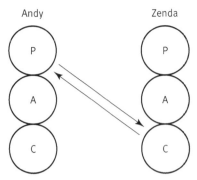

Andy   Zenda

'I'm disappointed you haven't managed to make any progress in getting the children to bed on time.'

'I'm really sorry. I really will do it this week. It is really hard.'

This type of transaction is where the ego-state addressed is the one which responds.

Figure 4.2 Complementary transaction

In the above transaction, Andy is making a statement from his Controlling Parent ego-state and this is directed at Zenda's Adapted Child ego-state. Zenda replies from her Child ego-state back to Andy's Parent ego-state. This constitutes what is called a *complementary transaction* (Berne, 1975, p14). Andy could then carry on the conversation with *well, you really must get them to bed on time* (Controlling Parent) and Zenda could continue with *I will, I promise I'll try again this week* (Adapted Child).

Engaging in complementary transactions keeps both parties in the same position. In the above example, this keeps Andy in a position of authority and keeps Zenda in a position of being controlled. Zenda dares not tell Andy she is not really sure how to implement the strategy and tries instead to placate him. This is not an effective position for either person and makes progress difficult.

Instead of replying from his Parent ego-state Andy could change direction and reply from his Adult ego-state. This would involve a crossed transaction, i.e. one where the ego-state addressed is not the one which responds (Stewart and Joines, 1987). Zenda is expecting a Parent reaction but Andy realises this is not working and chooses to respond from his Adult ego-state instead. This crossed transaction would look like the following:

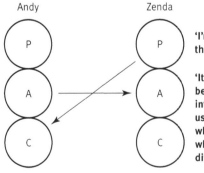

Andy   Zenda

'I'm really sorry. I really will do it this week.

'It sounds as if the strategies have been a real challenge for you to put into practice. Would it be useful for us both to have a closer look at what you did well this week and what you could have done a little differently?'

Figure 4.3 Crossed transaction

If Andy uses an Adult statement he is more likely to elicit an Adult response from Zenda. In this instance Zenda might reply by saying the following:

> *That's a relief. I was worried about telling you I wasn't really sure how to go about this. Breaking it down into smaller steps would really help me to get this right.*

Because Zenda is now enabled to speak openly, the communication reverts to a complementary transaction (Adult to Adult). In this scenario, this is a much healthier position than one which consists of Parent to Child transactions.

Game-playing and game analysis

Another type of interaction that takes place is called an *ulterior transaction*. In these sorts of conversations, what seems to be taking place on the surface is not what is really going on underneath. In other words, there are deeper levels of unconscious processes at work. When this happens, says Berne (1971), a game is likely to be taking place. According to Karpman (1968), game-playing involves the participants adopting one of three roles: Persecutor, Rescuer or Victim, with the participants switching from one position to another, for example from Victim to Persecutor. Karpman called this the *Drama Triangle*.

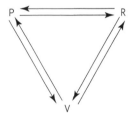

Figure 4.4 Karpman's Drama Triangle (Stephen B Karpman, M.D., 1968)

Stewart and Joines (1987) state that when the Drama Triangle is at play, all the participants are responding to their past rather than what is really happening in the present. Berne (1964) states that people play games in this way in order to experience an old, recognisable feeling which is rarely comfortable, but nevertheless familiar. This is usually unconscious and not often deliberate.

CASE STUDY

Let us illustrate game-playing and the Drama Triangle by looking at the case example of Joey. Joey is 18 years old and after years of living in children's homes and failed foster placements is finally living in his own flat. For six months he has been in a relationship with a young woman, Gina. After their first big argument, Gina walks out and Joey does not know where she has gone. Gary is his social worker and during a visit he talks to him about this. Unwittingly, Gary begins a game called 'Why Don't You, Yes But...' (Berne, 1964).

Continued

Gary: *Joey, why don't you text or ring her to find out what is happening?* (Rescuer).

Joey: *Yes, but she wouldn't reply, there's no point, she's really gone off me* (Victim).

Gary: *I'm sure that's not the case. Why don't you contact one of her friends to and ask them to pass a message on to her?* (Rescuer).

Joey: *Yes, but all her friends hate me and can't understand what she sees in me* (Victim).

Gary: *You could contact her mum and find out if she's gone home* (Rescuer).

Joey: *She hates me too* (Victim). *Anyway, I've told you, there's no point and you're not listening to me. I thought you could help me – but you're useless* (switches from Victim to Persecutor).

Gary: *Oh, sorry, I can't think what else to suggest* (switches from Rescuer to Victim).

Both Gary and Joey have switched around the Drama Triangle and finish the transaction experiencing an old, familiar feeling. Joey's unconscious process is related to his reaction to numerous rejections and moves within the care system. He feels he is unlovable and that consequently it is inevitable that any girlfriend will leave him. He therefore thinks there is no point in contacting Gina because, in his mind, he cannot understand why she would possibly want to come back to him.

Gary, on the other hand, might not be very confident in his ability to help anyone because of messages he received in his own childhood about not being good enough. Both participants switch into different positions on the Drama Triangle and end experiencing feelings with which they are both familiar.

Berne (1964) states that in order to overcome the barriers inherent in this type of game, one person (in this case Gary) needs to take the lead and remove himself from playing the Rescuer, Victim or Persecutor and to take an Adult position. If he were to do this, instead of saying to Joey why don't you *he could instead say* OK Joey, what do you need to do to resolve this? *Making an Adult response can invite Joey to leave the Drama Triangle and respond from his Adult ego-state himself. In the Adult ego-state Joey might then say* I need to find out whether or not it is definitely over.

Revisit activity 4.5 and think about the unconscious processes that were taking place.

- *How might you and the other person have adopted the position of Persecutor, Victim or Rescuer?*
- *Did a switch take place and, if so, what position did you both switch to?*
- *What were the underlying feelings you were left with?*
- *Were these familiar feelings?*
- *How could you have stepped off the Drama Triangle and used your Adult ego-state to encourage a better outcome?*

COMMENT

Berne (1964, p44) describes a game as an ongoing series of complementary ulterior transactions progressing to a well-defined, predictable outcome. *If we can begin to work out our unconscious processes and what is really happening between ourselves and others, then we will be much better placed to remove these ensuing barriers to good communication. This is a lifelong process and one which requires constant monitoring by ourselves, both during our interactions and afterwards in supervision.*

Learning about Transactional Analysis and game-playing then, can help us to explore our unconscious processes which can become barriers to engaging. Of course, the temptation when practising these concepts is to focus on the other person's behaviour and not our own. As Burgess (2005) states, Transactional Analysis and the Drama Triangle should be used as a tool to help us to gain self-knowledge and change our *own* behaviour rather than to criticise others. This is a very important point. Using Transactional Analysis as a tool for self-development will help us to remove the barriers which arise from our unconscious processes.

CHAPTER SUMMARY

When we first start to think about barriers to engaging with service-users, it is tempting to focus only on level one barriers. My experience from teaching is that the students who have the most to learn tend to be the ones who focus most on barriers such as placing a desk or table in front of the service-user or whether or not they are sitting correctly or playing with their pen. While we definitely need to have awareness of and eliminate such level one barriers, we need also to focus on those which inhibit a deeper level of engagement. Being aware of and eliminating level two barriers requires us to recognise that engaging with service-users is a joint enterprise and we need to underpin our skills with theoretical ways of working. Using theory encourages us to develop conscious awareness of what we are doing and why we are doing it; for example, if we understand that Rogers' person-centred theory (1961) places the service-user in charge of their own decision making then we will be less tempted to take over and tell the person what to do. Level three barriers are the hardest to overcome because eliminating these requires us to be willing to develop a deeper level of self-knowledge. We need to be aware of our underpinning values and our long-standing patterns of communication. We also need to be prepared to change our ways of communicating when they are not working and to be able to think of how we could communicate differently. All of this requires a willingness on our part to identify and explore our patterns of behaviour and to practise different ways of working. We also need to recognise that this is a lifelong process and one which we will always have to monitor, both in supervision and in our day-to-day interactions.

Burgess, R (2005) A model for enhancing individual and organisational learning of 'emotional intelligence': The drama and winner's triangles. *Social Work Education*, 24 (1): 97–112.

This is a humorous and very interesting article on how social work practitioners can use Karpman's Drama Triangle in everyday interactions with service-users.

Berne, E (1975) *What do you say after you say hello?* London: Corgi.

Berne writes with an engaging and easy-to-read style about his theory of Transactional Analysis. Part one, General considerations, describes ego-states and Part two, Parental programming, explores how our early experiences influence our interactions as adults.

de Board, R (1997) *Counselling for toads*. London: Routledge.

In this humorous and easy-to-read book de Board imagines Toad (from Kenneth Grahame's *Wind in the Willows*) undergoes counselling from a Transactional Analysis perspective to help him overcome his depression.

Jacobs, M (2010) *Psychodynamic counselling in action*. 4th edition. London: Sage.

Chapter 1 defines transference and counter-transference and Chapter 6 gives case examples of working with these concepts.

Stewart, I and Joines, V (1987) *TA today: A new introduction to transactional analysis*. Nottingham: Lifespace Publishing.

This is a detailed and readable text, which gives the reader both a theoretical and practical understanding of Transactional Analysis. It is also packed full with self-development exercises. Chapters 1 to 6 focus on ego-states.

Chapter 5
Using challenging skills to raise concerns

Introduction

A major task in social work is the requirement to challenge people and raise concerns when necessary. Challenging effectively requires practise and skill. It is easy to get it wrong and the consequences of poor challenging can be at best a real knock to the social work relationship and at worst lead to a violent reaction from the recipient. There is little research into what constitutes effective challenging in social work but counselling skills have much to teach us in this area. Effective challenging helps the service-user to see themselves and their situation a little differently and precedes the process of change. Challenge should always be conducted in an empathic, non-judgemental but nevertheless clear and sometimes firm manner and it is this combination of requirements which makes it a difficult skill to learn. In this chapter we will explore particular skills which may help us to challenge effectively.

So far, the process of using counselling skills discussed in earlier chapters has involved building relationships by actively listening to service-users and trying to establish what is going on for them. The service-user has led the way here. Now, when challenging is used, the control of the content of the sessions is moved more into the practitioner's domain (Taylor, 1998; Nelson-Jones, 2008).

According to Nelson-Jones (2008), encouraging service-users to change involves challenging discrepancies in feelings, thinking and behaviour. Egan (1977, 1994 and 2010) writes extensively about what to challenge and how to do it effectively and has expanded his work in this area with each edition of *The skilled helper*. In this chapter we will be exploring challenging skills from Egan's model and other theories such as assertiveness. Lishman (2009) has applied Egan's work on challenging skills to social work situations and this chapter will build on Lishman's work by further applying techniques of challenging to social work case examples.

Pitfalls in challenging

So far in this book, we have explored how using counselling skills in social work places the service-user at the centre of decision making and indeed the helping process. Using challenging skills and raising concerns is no different. Poor challenging involves being brusque, controlling and often contains a *'you must do this or else'* approach. However, when we are on the receiving end of this kind of intervention, our reaction can be one of stubbornness. Try the following activity.

ACTIVITY **5.1**

Think of the last time someone gave you strong and brusque feedback about one of your shortcomings.

- *What effect did the person's manner have on you?*

- *How willing were you to change your behaviour as a result of the feedback?*

COMMENT

It is likely that the more you were told off about your weaknesses, the more you demonstrated one of the following reactions:

- *You refused to agree, even if the other person was right.*

- *You dug your heels in and refused to change.*

- *You felt demeaned and embarrassed and wanted to get away from the other person.*

- *You felt angry and wanted to get your own back.*

- *You disengaged.*

These are common reactions to harsh challenging and service-users will be no different in their responses if you use such an approach.

Effective challenging skills

As we have seen in previous chapters, to become effective practitioners, social work-ers need to build good working relationships with service-users. We have already seen that one way this can be achieved is to use counselling and person-centred skills which involve empathy, congruence, unconditional positive regard and a range of listening and engaging skills. However, Egan (2010) argues that empathic responding is not enough on its own to effect change. He states that practitioners also need to assist service-users to change their patterns of thinking, feeling and behaviour where these are destructive, self-defeating or keep landing them in trouble. Raising concerns is a key element of social work practice and learning to do this in a clear, assertive, empathic yet congruent manner is crucial to effective practice. Learning to challenge well assists practitioners in raising concerns. This chapter explores various techniques which will help in this process.

Techniques of challenging

Developing challenging skills requires self-awareness, assertiveness and lots of practise. The following techniques, all from Egan (2010 and 1994) and some developed by Lishman (2009), can really help you to hone your skills.

Earn the right to challenge

First of all, states Egan (2010, p253) practitioners need to *earn the right to challenge*. This means you need to establish a good, working relationship with the person first. You need to be open to challenge yourself and willing to explore your own style of challenging. Before making any intervention, use something called your *internal supervisor* (Casement, 1985, p30). This means imagining yourself in the shoes of the other person and seeing how you might react to the challenge about to be offered. All the skills you have already developed are used when challenging. Therefore, you continue to be empathic, use your active listening skills and remain respectful at all times. Remaining empathic makes it much more likely that your challenge will be heard and accepted.

Encourage service-users to challenge themselves

If you can prompt service-users to challenge themselves, this is the most effective form of challenge. Egan (2010) states that good challenging is about helping people to develop alternative perspectives and the more this can come from within rather than being told by another, the more likely change is to be sustained. Imagine you are working with the following person.

CASE STUDY

Karen, aged 28, is a single parent seeking help for her dependency on heroin. She has attended a rehabilitation programme on two previous occasions but each time has returned to using drugs. This time, she says, it will be different but you notice all her close friendships are with other drug users. Karen has a six-year-old daughter, Jade, who is living

Continued

---

at home with her. Jade is subject to a child protection plan because of Karen's neglect and emotional unavailability. If you were working with Karen, who is now seeking help for drug dependency, you might offer the following prompts to help her challenge herself:

I can see it is really hard for you to stop using drugs Karen but I wonder what you think the effect of continuing to do this is having on your relationship with Jade.

It must be hard to break old habits when lots of people around you are also using drugs. I'm wondering what impact this will have on you being able to stop.

As Karen's social worker, you have noticed her life still revolves around drug-taking activities. Inviting Karen to examine what she is doing will focus her on exploring the difference between what she hopes for and what might happen in reality. If she can make this link herself, she is more likely to do something about it. Also, inviting Karen to think about how her drug taking affects Jade is likely to have a greater impact than you telling her directly.

Focus on service-users' strengths rather than weaknesses and build on their successes

A number of authors highlight the importance of encouraging service-users to focus on what they are doing well or have done well in the past (Milner and O'Byrne, 2009; Lindsay, 2009; Lishman, 2009; Koprowska, 2003; Hanna et al., 1999; Egan, 2010; Egan, 1977). Pointing out to service-users their skills and inner strengths helps to build confidence and encourages change and action. The temptation as a social worker is to focus on people's weaknesses and tell them what they could have done differently. Service-users may be used to getting negative feedback and as a consequence feel distrustful of social workers and lack self-esteem. Being critical further demolishes trust and confidence. Try the following activity.

ACTIVITY 5.2

Work in a trio: you are to act as a service-user. Ask your two colleagues to act as helper and observer. Talk to the helper for five minutes about an event you found difficult to handle. Ask the helper to first focus on the weaknesses you displayed during your managing of this event. Next, ask the helper to instead focus on and give you feedback on the strengths you showed in dealing with the situation. Ask the observer for feedback and then discuss with both people the effect each approach had on you. If you would prefer to work on your own, assess your own weaknesses and strengths demonstrated during the event.

COMMENT

It is likely that when the helper gave you feedback on your weaknesses, first you did not hear anything for which you had not previously berated yourself. Second, it is likely that you felt embarrassed, judged and de-motivated. When the helper focused on your strengths and helped you build on your successes, it is likely you felt more energised and motivated to do things differently next time. If you assessed your own weaknesses and strengths, it is likely that similar feelings became apparent to you.

Respect service-users' values

First of all we need to understand our own value system and recognise where it differs from that of the service-user. Warren (2007, p73) states this is important because *it helps us guard against manipulation and control so that we can more readily empower service-users*. We need to be careful when challenging that we are not simply imposing our values on the service-user. It would be easy to say to Karen (from the case study above) *you need to stop taking drugs, it is really bad for your health and you aren't meeting Jade's needs* if we would not consider taking drugs ourselves. However, neither does respecting values mean agreeing with the other person. A much more productive approach is to help Karen to explore how her values regarding drugs are driving her behaviour. For example, your challenge could be:

> *Karen, I can see you really want to stop using heroin, but from what I can see, your whole life and the people you socialise with are heavily steeped in a culture of drug use. It might be useful to explore how remaining in this culture is affecting you and your relationship with Jade.*

Be tentative but not apologetic

The Oxford English Dictionary defines the word *tentative* as an *experimental proposal, trial or theory*. Egan (2010, p253) describes being tentative as an approach *which invites co-operation* rather than *arouses resistance*. At the same time, it is important not to be apologetic in your approach otherwise the other person will not take any notice of your intervention. Examples of tentative challenges include the following:

- *What occurs to me is coming off drugs will leave a big hole in your social life.*

- *It seems to me...*

- *My observations are...*

- *What I am noticing is...*

- *I am wondering whether...*

- *From where I am sitting it appears...*

- *I am wondering if you can see it from your daughter's point of view. How do you think she is affected by your drug taking?*

Being tentative then involves posing a topic for debate. As the social worker, you need to demonstrate a curiosity about what is happening for the service-user and be genuinely interested in helping them to expand their view. Also, the way you challenge needs to use vocabulary and language that come naturally to you: it is about finding ways of being tentative which fit in with the way you normally speak.

Be specific and clear

It is important to be clear and specific because the service-user is more likely to hear your challenge, understand exactly what you are saying and engage with you in response (Egan, 2010). Dickson (2000) in discussing assertive approaches highlights the importance of being specific. She writes about making clear statements rather than asking wishy-washy questions which could be interpreted ambiguously. This way the other person understands completely the point you are making. Let us suppose your invitation for Karen to challenge herself regarding her care of Jade has fallen on deaf ears.

> **Karen:** *Jade has always been OK and we will manage just the same as we always have done.*

Karen is not looking at the consequences of her behaviour and is finding it hard to challenge herself. Here, you would need to make the challenge yourself by raising the concern in a specific and clear manner.

> **You:** *Karen, I can see how much you love Jade but I have a real concern that your continued drug taking means you are not always able to take care of her in the way that you need to.*

Acknowledge and deal caringly with defensiveness

Being challenged is difficult for all of us. Think back to activity 5.1 and remember your initial response when someone gave you feedback that was difficult to hear. Egan (2010) tells us not to be surprised when service-users react strongly to our challenges. We need to anticipate such reactions and work with them. Imagine you are working with the following person.

CASE STUDY

Donna, 22, is a single parent with a four-year-old daughter, Maddie. She has no family of her own. After several years alone she has begun a relationship with Eddie, 37. He is on the Sex Offenders' Register after serving a prison sentence for making and sending pornographic images of children via his computer. Donna is completely besotted with Eddie.

If you were working with Donna, your interaction might progress on the following lines:

> **You:** I know it has been very hard for you: you have been on your own for a long time and have now met someone who seems to be doing lots for you. I'm finding it hard to find the right way to say this but I need to tell you that I am very worried about Eddie's past offending behaviour. He has a history of harming children and I am concerned that Maddie is at risk.

> **Donna:** Eddie is the best thing that has happened to me in a long time. Other people had access to his computer. There is no proof it was him, he just carried the can for whoever did it.

It would be easy at this point to become judgemental and directive towards Donna and say, Donna, you need to wake up to reality. Stop this relationship or else we will need to take action. *While you need to be clear with Donna, you first need to deal with her defensiveness. You could try the following approach:*

> **You:** Because Eddie has been so nice to you it is hard for you to see this other, more hidden side to his character. You may be telling yourself it could not possibly have been him that did these things.

Continued

Donna: But he is a really nice person. He would not have done that...

You: I know it is really difficult for you to believe what I am saying and I'm finding it uncomfortable to say these things because I know you are feeling very happy and positive for the first time in a long time. But Eddie did do these things. It is still hard for you to believe the truth because you yourself have only seen him being good to you. But there is another side to him Donna and I am really worried for both you and Maddie.

Working with the person's defensiveness first means thinking about why they might be defensive in the first place. Doing this takes us back to a skill developed in previous chapters and which should underpin all interactions: using empathy. The role of using empathy in challenging will be discussed next.

Continue to use empathy and follow your hunches

It is important when challenging to remember that empathy, congruence and unconditional positive regard need to underpin your skills. In the examples given so far you can see an effective approach is to put yourself in the service-user's position. Donna is lonely and isolated. She has now met someone who is giving her lots of attention and she feels cared for: something she has really missed. Of course she will find it very difficult to see the worrying aspects of Eddie. Neither will it cross her mind that she may be being groomed. Inviting Donna to challenge herself might also be useful here:

You: *Donna, imagine a good friend of yours was in the same position as you. After years of being on her own, she meets a new man who is being really good to her. He is telling her his conviction for sex offences was not his fault. She has a daughter the same age as Maddie. What would you say to her?*

Donna: *I'd tell her to be careful, all may not be as it seemed. I would worry he was being nice to her for a reason...*

You: *You would worry he was getting into her good books in order to get access to her daughter.*

Donna: *Yes, I would...*

Helping service-users to make the connections themselves can have more far-reaching and long-lasting effects than simply telling them directly. If the person finds it hard to challenge themselves or does not want to engage with you in this process you would need to try using more direct skills such as the *Three-line Strategy* outlined below. An important point is to always make sure your challenges employ empathic responses. One way to do this is to identify and share your hunches. According to Egan (2010), sharing your hunches can help the service-user to see the bigger picture, begin to make links and open up thoughts and feelings which up to now they have successfully ignored. Once the person begins to make realistic connections, they are more likely to identify themes and move to action. One hunch you might have about Donna is why she is drawn so strongly to Eddie and how adept he is at grooming. Bringing your hunch out into the open and helping Donna to make the connections can challenge her to see things more realistically. At the same time you need to be careful not to destroy the confidence she has in herself and to build her self-esteem:

> **You:** *Donna, it's really hard for you because you see Eddie being really nice and think 'how could someone who is this good to me have done these things to children?'*

> **Donna:** *But he is a really nice person, he brings me flowers, he takes me out and he's really good to me and Maddie. I haven't had that in a long time.*

> **You:** *You have felt very lonely and missed someone caring for you and then Eddie comes along. When he is being so attentive it is hard for you to see him as anything other than a nice man. However, my experience is that people like Eddie are very skilled at hiding their real motives by appearing to be caring and considerate. My worry is that this is happening with you and Maddie and that you have let him convince you all is well.*

> **Donna:** *I can't believe he's really like that. Or maybe I don't want to believe it.*

> **You:** *It's absolutely understandable. You're finding it hard to admit you have let him persuade you that he really didn't do it. But I can also see that you are acknowledging what I am saying about him is true.*

Remaining respectful and empathic throughout and at the same time gently but clearly helping the service-user to realise the reality of the situation is one way of raising this concern. If Donna can be supported to make the links and connections herself, then there is a greater likelihood of a positive outcome, i.e. for her to end the relationship. In the above examples there is a sustained focus on Donna's thoughts and behaviour rather than Eddie's. The social worker does not say *Eddie has persuaded you*, rather, she says *you have let him persuade you*. There is an important distinction to be made in the semantics of the language here. *Eddie has persuaded you* leaves the fault and action with Eddie, which cannot be changed. Donna cannot change Eddie, but by seeing that she has *chosen* to let herself be persuaded by Eddie, she can choose an alternative form of behaviour, i.e. to not be persuaded by him and thus do something different such as end the relationship.

Remember that at all times, your challenge needs to be linked to action (Egan, 2010) and to move the service-user in the direction of managing their issues and problems more positively. Sometimes you will be doing all you can to challenge the person yet they find it difficult to engage. A final technique you could try in this situation is discussed next.

Raising concerns and taking action: Using the three-line strategy

Assertiveness techniques will be discussed in more detail in Chapter 8 but it is timely here to look at a particular assertiveness skill called the Three-line Strategy (Smith, 1975; Jeffers, 2007), which is useful in both challenging and raising concerns. This technique is described as follows:

1. **Let the other person know you are listening and that you appreciate their position**. In other words, use your empathy skills to demonstrate you are trying to understand what it might be like for the other person. You can use phrases such as:

I realise that…

I can see that you…

It must be difficult for you when…

2. **State how you feel or what you think.** Here, it is important to actually use the word 'I'. This is not suggesting you bare your soul about your feelings. Rather it is inviting you to be congruent about what is going on for you. You could try variations of the following statements:

I'm finding it uncomfortable to say this…

I feel frustrated because…

I feel I have no alternative…

I feel torn because…

I feel caught between the devil and the deep blue sea.

I think this is impossible to resolve to everyone's satisfaction so…

I think a decision needs to be made.

I feel we have reached an impasse…

I feel frustrated because all the ways forward we have discussed have been rejected. Therefore I need to say…

3. **State what you want/would like to happen/action you will take.** This needs to be clearly and directly stated. You need to take a deep breath and say it as it is while at the same time remaining respectful towards the service-user:

What I would like to happen is…

What I am going to do is…

I want…

I need…

Let us try this technique with Karen.

CASE STUDY

Returning to Karen, imagine that you have done your best to use challenging skills discussed earlier in this chapter. During your interactions with Karen you have noticed several themes. Karen has tried before to stop taking heroin but has not managed to sustain her withdrawal. She is having a relationship with another drug user and her friends also take drugs. She has responsibility for Jade, her six-year-old daughter, whom you are worried about. You have tried hard to help Karen to challenge herself about the consequences of her drug dependency and you have confronted her more directly yourself. Karen has not responded to these approaches so now you feel the need to be more direct and choose to use the Three-line Strategy:

Continued

1. *Karen, I can see how much you love Jade and how being parted from her would be painful for you. I can also see that you have tried to give up heroin before several times so I know you want to do this. (This lets Karen know you are listening and that you appreciate her position.)*

2. *I feel uncomfortable saying this to you because we have built a good and honest relationship over the time we have been meeting. I think it has been really difficult for you to stop taking and stay off heroin because you surround yourself with other users. I worry about your ability to care for Jade because my observations are you have not addressed this issue. I feel that although you say you are going to stop, in reality this is hard for you to put into practice because it is difficult for you to take yourself out of the drug environment you are in. I have serious concerns about your ability to care for Jade. (You are stating what you feel and think.)*

3. *Because I have been unable to help you to see and address these concerns, I have no choice but to arrange a case conference to discuss Jade's future care. (You are being clear about the action you will take.)*

Using the Three-line Strategy well will involve all of the skills already developed in both this and previous chapters. It is important to remain respectful, empathic and to own the assertions being made (using 'I' statements such as I worry about...my observations are...I have serious concerns about...). You are making a judgement about what needs to happen while at the same time avoiding judgemental remarks towards Karen. This technique helps you to encourage Karen to see how her own actions have contributed to the outcome. You do not fall into the trap of saying you shouldn't have...or it is your own fault....which would leave Karen more likely to respond from her Child ego-state and so get into an argument with you. By using 'I' statements, you remain in the Adult position and invite an Adult response.

Imagine you are the child protection social worker involved with Donna and her four-year-old daughter, Maddie, whom we met earlier. You have done your best to help Donna challenge herself about the consequences of remaining in a relationship with Eddie, her 37-year-old boyfriend who has convictions for making and sending pornographic images of children on his computer. You have helped her to look at her blind spots and how she is keeping herself in the dark about the reality of the situation. Donna has refused to engage with the seriousness of her position and now, you have no alternative but to state clearly to her the action you are going to take. You decide to do this using the Three-line Strategy. Remember you will try and do this with empathy, congruence and by remaining non-judgemental towards Donna.

- *What would you say to demonstrate you are trying to see the situation from Donna's point of view?*
- *How would you communicate what you feel or think?*
- *How would you raise your concern and state what might happen?*

COMMENT

It is important that you use words and vocabulary that are familiar to you and with which you feel comfortable. Try to avoid confrontational statements such as if you don't stop this relationship immediately... *Using the Three-line Strategy your response might be along the following lines:*

> Donna, I can see how lonely you have been and how Eddie's presence is filling a huge void in your life. However, I feel very concerned about Maddie's safety because you are choosing to continue a relationship with Eddie who is a risk to children and by doing this you are putting Maddie at grave risk of harm. I feel frustrated because we don't seem to be moving on from here. I am now so concerned, a case conference will have to be arranged. Here, legal advice will be sought to begin legal proceedings to protect Maddie.

You would still maintain an empathic approach, trying to understand what all of this might be like for Donna. You can see she is vulnerable herself and that she will have low self-esteem. Continuing to help her recognise and work on this may yet still bring about a more positive conclusion.

Key areas where challenging is useful

We need to recognise situations, points of view and ways of behaving that might benefit from challenging. Egan's various editions of *The skilled helper* (1994, 2007, 2010) state that challenging is useful in the following areas:

- Failure to own problems or define them in solvable terms.

- Discrepancies, evasions, distortions and game-playing including self-deception and choosing to stay in the dark.

- Simple unawareness.

- Blind spots, excuses and failure to care about the consequences of behaviour.

These areas will now be explored further and applied to social work case examples.

Failure to own problems or define them in solvable terms

According to Egan (2010), we are all quite accomplished at avoiding taking responsibility for ourselves, our decisions and our behaviour. It is easier to blame others than to look at what we could do differently. Berne (1975) writes that we live in a 'make do' world where we might say *he made me stay at home and look after him rather than get a job* or *she made me angry* or *if my parents had looked after me properly when I was a child I wouldn't be behaving like this now*. Berne's attitude is that even though we may feel *compelled* to act or think in a certain way, how we think or behave always involves a *choice* of any number of actions. The following example illustrates this.

Matt

Matt, 15, is displaying increasingly violent and out of control behaviour. Last week he punched his mother, Anne, when she tried to get him out of bed to go to school. Matt talks to you, his social worker, about his anger.

Matt: She just goes on and on at me the whole time. She's always on my case, nag, nag, nag. Clean your bedroom. Go to school. She doesn't give me a minute's peace. She winds me up and makes me angry. If she stopped going on at me, I wouldn't react like I do.

Matt is saying here it is not his fault he gets angry, rather it is his mum's fault and that his behaviour is a result of what his mum does or does not do. He is saying she made me angry. *Berne (1975) would say that Matt is* choosing *to react in this way. When he feels his mum is 'nagging' him, he could choose any number of different reactions. He could:*

- *not respond at all;*

- *get down on the floor and have a tantrum;*

- *leave the room;*

- *laugh;*

- *stay calm and think about how he could react;*

- *say:* I know you want me to do this but I don't feel like it now;

- *say:* OK, I'll do it now;

- *say:* if you stop nagging me, I'll do it;

- *listen to his mum, acknowledge what she is saying and choose what he is going to do/not do.*

If Matt can see it is not his mum making him angry but that he, albeit at an unconscious level is choosing to get angry, then he can choose an alternative form of behaviour and thus take ownership of his own actions. If you were working with Matt, you could challenge him about all the ways he could choose to respond:

You: Matt, I can see you feel angry when you feel pushed into doing things you do not want to do and that you feel it is not possible to control how you respond. But we can work out together what it is that is influencing your angry response. I wonder what happens inside you when you hear your mum's words and what it is that influences you to give such an angry reaction?

The thinking behind this response is to try and encourage Matt to see that he could choose to interpret his mother's words and requests differently, especially if he was able to look beyond his feelings to her motivations. Once Matt has stopped blaming his mum for 'making' him angry, he will be able to see that he can take charge of himself and choose a different response.

Discrepancies, evasions, distortions and game-playing including self-deception and choosing to stay in the dark

As practitioners, we will frequently come across all of the above forms of behaviour and need to be ready to challenge these appropriately. Lishman (2009, p181) states,

> *Discrepancies occur between verbal and non-verbal behaviour, between what we think or say and what we do, between our own views of ourselves and others' views.*

When we are raising concerns and challenging people, we need to be vigilant to the discrepancies and evasions we observe. For example, let us look at the following situation. Jenny, aged five, is sent home from school because she has scabies. The school has informed you that Jack, her father and main carer, has not responded to the school's request to take her to a doctor. When you visit, you find the house in a dirty and dishevelled state. When you talk to Jack he says he is coping fine and doesn't need any help. He says he will take Jenny to the doctor next week. You notice, when he says this, he looks at the floor and seems distracted. You sense from the discrepancies between his verbal and non-verbal communication that he is evading the issue. He may be embarrassed by Jenny's illness and may be avoiding taking her to the doctor's because he fears being blamed.

Self-deception is another area which requires challenge. Imagine Luke, aged 18, is in the process of leaving care and you are helping him to find a flat. He is looking forward to gaining some independence but you are concerned about his money management skills and how he will budget to pay his bills. You worry he is deceiving himself when he says he will not spend all his money in one go. However, you have witnessed him doing this with his leaving care grant. You would need to challenge Luke on how his good intentions may not actually happen in practice.

Game-playing has been discussed in detail in Chapter 4. Game-playing involves both parties adopting either a persecutor, victim or rescuing position and then switching positions on a drama triangle (Karpman, 1968). The key to challenging game-playing effectively is for us to acknowledge the role in the game that we are playing. For example, if I am playing a *Why Don't You, Yes But* game and making suggestions to the service-user, all of which are being rebutted, I need to recognise I am rescuing and that it is getting us both nowhere. The challenge would involve the practitioner saying *OK, what do you think your options are?* This would keep us both in the Adult ego-state.

Choosing to stay in the dark is where the person could find out information which would help them to face up to something but they choose not to do so. For example, Andrew, whose father died from bowel cancer, develops persistent diarrhoea but puts off going to his doctor because he fears the same fate. Challenging Andrew to face up to his fears and act now will mean any treatment needed is likely to be more effective.

Simple unawareness

Egan (2010) describes this as where a person engages in behaviour that has an effect on other people of which they are unaware or only vaguely aware. For example, Hazel attends parenting classes for help with her three-year-old twins. She says that while she used to get support from her sister, Maggie, lately Maggie has stopped inviting Hazel round to her house and she feels hurt by this withdrawal. It transpires the twins ran riot throughout Maggie's house during their last visit. Hazel never stops them from doing this in her own house and cannot understand why this would upset her sister. The challenge required here is clear: to help Hazel understand that her failure to control her daughters is affecting her relationship with Maggie.

Blind spots and failure to care about the consequences of behaviour

When people carry on engaging in destructive or self-defeating behaviour, even when they know they can change it, Egan (2010, p225) refers to this as having *blind spots*. Blind spots can lead people to make excuses for themselves. For example, Ian's father left home when Ian was seven. As an adult, Ian frequently gets himself into situations where he lets anger get the better of him and recently he has recently served a prison sentence for assaulting his wife when she threatened to leave him. He blames his anger on his father and says *if he hadn't left, I wouldn't behave like this now*. Ian's blind spot is that he is now an adult and can, if he wishes, choose to react differently. He can also take responsibility for his actions. In blaming his father, Ian is making excuses for his own behaviour. While he continues to do this, his behaviour is unlikely to change.

ACTIVITY 5.4

Think about the theory and techniques discussed in this chapter. How you would challenge Jack, Luke, Andrew, Hazel and Ian? Write down the dialogue you would actually use.

CHAPTER SUMMARY

As we have seen, challenging skills and raising concerns require many different skills if we are to accomplish them well. Your starting point is to use skills that are already familiar to you such as empathic responding, respect, congruence and unconditional positive regard. You then use some additional tools and attempt to invite service-users to challenge themselves. Then, you try gently challenging the person yourself, building up to being more direct and specific if your challenges are not getting through. Finally, employing assertiveness skills in the form of the Three-line Strategy can be used when all else has failed. Remaining compassionate and empathic while raising concerns can be difficult for us to do, but adopting this approach is the key to effective challenging. If we are to keep service-users at the centre of decision making and recognise that they are responsible for themselves, their actions and their destiny, then the skills you have developed in this chapter are essential.

FURTHER READING

Egan, G (2010) *The skilled helper: A problem management and opportunity development approach to helping.* 9th edition. Belmont, CA: Brooks/Cole.

Read Chapter 8, Stage 1: task 2 – *facilitate client self-challenge: from new perspectives to new behaviour*, pp210–42 and also Chapter 9, *Further thoughts on challenge*, pp243–57. Egan's analysis of challenging skills is absolutely excellent. He writes with clarity and illustrates his work with many case examples. Although the focus is on counselling, Egan's concepts can easily be applied to social work situations.

Lishman, J (2009) *Communication in social work*. 2nd edition. Basingstoke: Palgrave Macmillan.

This is an excellent book which helps practitioners to develop their communication skills. Chapter 9, Intervention: non-verbal and verbal techniques for enhancing behavioural and attitudinal change, contains some very helpful points on challenging in social work.

BBC (2004) *Assertiveness and assertiveness training* bbc.co.uk/dna/h2g2

Some useful assertiveness skills are described on this BBC website. We will be building on these skills in Chapter 8.

Chapter 6
Service-users managing their own lives

Introduction

So far in this book, we have explored the importance of building effective working relationships with service-users. We have seen how this process helps people to feel understood and better able to understand their own strengths and motives. This chapter builds on these skills and explores how we can help service-users to take control of their own lives by assisting them in determining what they want or need that will make a difference.

A paper by the Department for Children, Schools and Families in 2010 outlined the recommendations by the Social Work Task Force. Highlighted here was the importance of finding out what would help service-users and so, wherever possible, enable them to have as much control as possible over their lives:

Social workers can make life better for people in crisis who are struggling to cope, feel alone and cannot sort out their problems unaided. How social workers do this depends on the circumstances. Usually they work in partnership with the people they are supporting – check out what they need, find what will help them, build their confidence, and open doors to other services.

(DCSF, 2010, p19)

This chapter focuses on counselling skills which help us to work in partnership with service-users to establish their particular needs. Practical ways of helping people to identify and explore goals will be explored first. Then, strategies for achieving and adhering to goals will be discussed. The chapter draws from Egan's (2010) Skilled Helper model and from Wosket's (2006) interpretation of Egan's work. By the end of the chapter, you will have developed tools which will help you to enable service-users to say what they need so that they retain control in this area of their lives.

Establishing what service-users need

We can see from the Social Work Task Force Report that wherever it is possible, partnership working with service-users should be the aim in good social work practice. Warren (2007) highlights the value of a collaborative approach with service-users, emphasising the importance of their engagement in assessing situations and planning the delivery of services. O'Sullivan (2011, p46) argues that the aim of social work support is to help service-users to make informed decisions and that *there should be a presumption that service-users have the right and capacity to make decisions for themselves unless there are valid reasons for believing otherwise.* O'Sullivan also states that because practitioners sometimes have only a vague notion of what it actually means for service-users to have control over their own lives they can believe service-users are fully engaged in decision making when, in fact, they are not.

As practitioners, it is easy to think that we know what a service-user wants or needs, especially when we have taken time to listen to somebody exploring their current circumstances. Many people are attracted into social work because they want to help others and some believe such help consists of telling service-users how to overcome their difficulties. This approach is often carried out with the best of intentions, however, it does not lead to true partnership working where service-users are able to explore the best way forward for themselves. Each person with whom we work is a complete individual with a unique experience of life (Rogers, 1961) and what might work as a solution for me will not necessarily work for them. This point is as true for working with children as it is for adults. Indeed, Kirwan et al. (2004) cited in Warren (2007) found from their research with children that young people prefer to be asked what they want to do rather than practitioners guessing about this. O'Sullivan (2011) argues if service-users are to be in control of making informed decisions, practitioners need to know how to assist them in this process, for example by helping people to fully explore all available options as opposed to influencing their choices. To engage in a high level of partnership with the service-user, we first need to establish what their wishes are and then to elicit their ideas for how difficulties might be managed.

In some situations, of course, circumstances will dictate the extent of partnership working. O'Sullivan (2011) defines four levels of service-user involvement, and states that each level relates to specific decision situations rather than to the individual. These levels, from lowest to highest, are:

- being told (e.g. being informed of the result of a court order);

- being consulted (e.g. where the service-user's opinion is taken into account);

- being a partner (e.g. where decisions are jointly made);

- being in control (e.g. where the service-user makes decisions for themselves such as controlling a personalisation budget).

O'Sullivan emphasises that practitioners need to identify and work to the highest level of involvement that can be achieved.

Developing a high level of partnership working with service-users requires specific skills and this chapter focuses on the skills which will enable the service-user to be in control of decision making. In previous chapters, we have explored how using skills from stage one of the Egan model (2010) can help us to engage with and challenge service-users. Using stages two and three of Egan's model can help us to establish clearly the service-user's wants and needs. We will begin with a description of stage two, *the preferred picture*.

RESEARCH SUMMARY

Egan model stage two, the preferred picture

Egan (2010) states that all work with service-users needs to be solution focused, i.e. constantly moving towards action which will help the person to feel better and in more control of what is happening to them. Wosket (2006, p68) describes stage two as:

> ...helping clients turn their attention from examining their current difficulties and missed opportunities to imagining what the future could hold if their difficulties were eased or their opportunities seized.

Wosket (2006) acknowledges that because service-users have often lived with their difficulties for a long time they are consequently familiar with their day-to-day problems. She notes also that something less familiar to people is imagining what might constitute a better future. Thinking in this way can help the person to look ahead and make better decisions. Wosket states that an aim for practitioners is to help the service-user to move into stage two sooner rather than later, because establishing better possibilities helps the service-user to gain or re-kindle hope for the future.

There are three steps in Egan's stage two and Wosket (2006, p69) describes these succinctly in the following memorable way:

2A What do you want?

2B What do you really want?

2C Is what you really want what you are willing to pay for?

This chapter will explore these steps in more detail. In step 2A we begin by asking the person what they would like to happen that might improve their lives. In step 2B we help the person to explore how realistic and achievable are their desires (including assessing the resource implications). In step 2C we invite the person to look at what they might have to give up if they were to achieve their desire. We will explore each of these stages more thoroughly in this chapter.

Step 2A: What does the service-user want or need? Possibilities for a better future

During a workshop led by Egan, which I attended at the University of Hull in 1996, he said that he developed this aspect of his model after overhearing a conversation in a restaurant. A man was talking about his marriage problems and eventually the listener said 'Well, if your relationship was just what you wanted it to be, what would that look like?' This question is a prime example of how the speaker can be invited to begin to look at what possibilities they might have for a better world. The important factor here when helping is not to suggest solutions. Instead, the service-user needs to be invited to look at what might make things a little better. Service-users are not committing themselves at this point, rather they are exploring possibilities for a better future.

During my first contact with the Egan model, I found this stage difficult to use. What helped me was learning some easy to remember *future possibility* questions which invite the service-user to think about what would help them. For many months I had the following questions (all now adapted from Egan, 2010) written down as primers:

- What would help you most at the moment?

- How would you like things to be?

- If your life was just a little bit better, what would be happening that is not happening now?

- If you were managing a little better, what would be in place that is not in place now?

- What would you like to be doing differently with the people in your life?

- If your life was more as you wanted it, what would this look like?

- What do you want your life to be like in, say, six months/a year's time?

- If this situation stays the same, what would your life be like, say, in six months/a year's time?

- If you developed this opportunity, what would your life look like in the future?

- Can you think back to a time in your life when you felt happier/more confident/more in control? What was happening then that is not happening now?

ACTIVITY 6.1

Look at the list above of future possibility questions. It is important that we use our own vocabulary when we ask these questions.

- *For each question, decide if you could ask it in a different way that might be more comfortable for you.*

- *Add more future possibility questions that you can think of.*

COMMENT

Finding a way of using future possibility questions that is comfortable for you is important. Asking these types of questions keeps the responsibility for decision making with the service-user and limits the temptation of telling the person what to do. Keep a list of useful questions to hand and practise using them.

The following case study demonstrates how stage 2A questions can be used to help a service-user to explore a better future.

CASE STUDY

Carol

Carol is 26 years old and has been married to Ray for five years. They do not have any children. Imagine you are a hospital social worker. Carol first came to your attention a week ago when she was admitted with a fractured jaw and concussion. During your last conversation, Carol tells you that Ray caused her injuries by punching her in the face when he lost his temper during a drinking session. She says Ray is blaming stress at work for his behaviour and is very sorry for what he has done. He is telling her he will sort out his job, is begging her to come home and promising never to hurt her again. You have spent some time with Carol using empathic responses to build a relationship with her. You have learned that although this is not the first time she has been assaulted, it is the worst. She still loves Ray, however, she does not know whether or not to believe his promises. You decide to use an empathic response and to follow this with a future possibilities question:

> **You:** Because you love Ray you desperately want to believe him when he says he will sort out his issues at work and that he won't hurt you again. But what is making you question his promise is the fact that this is not the first time he has assaulted you and the violence is increasing each time. (*Empathic response.*) I'd just like to ask you about your own needs in all of this. What would help you most at the moment? (*Future possibilities question.*)

> **Carol:** I think what would help me most is some time on my own to recover in peace and to think properly about what I want. My mum wants me to go and stay with her when I come out of hospital and I am beginning to think this might be a good idea, at least in the short term.

Continued

CASE STUDY *continued*

You: You feel under pressure to respond to Ray's wishes and go home. However, what you really want is some breathing space and you feel the only way you can have this is to be away from him at the moment. It sounds as if going to your mum's would give you some peace and quiet and the opportunity to get back in touch with what your needs are. (*Further empathic response.*)

It is important to remember to give an empathic response after asking a future possibilities question. This way, Carol will be able to hear clearly what she has implied and also for her to feel you are fully engaging with her.

ACTIVITY 6.2

Think of a dilemma you are experiencing or a decision you need to make. Have a look at the list of future possibility questions above and either:

- *ask yourself one or two of the questions which strike you as being appropriate; or*

- *ask a friend or colleague to choose questions from the list to ask you which are relevant to your dilemma;*

- *assess whether or not the question assisted you to explore your dilemma/decision.*

COMMENT

Applying future possibility questions to ourselves can help us to take a look at what would help us the most and assist us in assessing what we really need. Thinking in this way also helps us to formulate specific goals. Once we have learned the value of working on ourselves in this way, we will be able to see how useful the technique is for working with service-users.

The magic wand question

Another *future possibilities* question Egan (2010) writes about asking is one called the *magic wand question*. This question is asked in the following way:

- If you could wave a magic wand and have what you wanted, what would that be?

It is important to follow up this question with the following probe:

- …and what would that do for you?

The following example illustrates using the *magic wand question*:

Service-user: *If I could wave a magic wand and have what I wanted it would be to win the lottery.*

Practitioner: *So if you won the lottery, what would that do for you?* (Probe.)

Service-user: *I would buy myself a desert island. It would have a draw-bridge to the mainland but I would keep it firmly up.*

Practitioner: *So what you really need at the moment is some time to yourself. It sounds as if you also want to find ways of obtaining some respite from people who are making demands on you. Having the equivalent of a drawbridge would leave you in charge of who you see and when you see them.* (Empathic response.)

Asking *and what would that do for you* helps the person to get in touch with what they really want and usually produces something realistically attainable. The service-user above is more likely to be struck by lightning than to win the lottery. However, asking the follow-up question helps him to identify his underlying desire, which is to have time to himself away from others' demands. His wish transpires to be both concrete and attainable and you can then work on this together.

It is very important to carry on using empathic responding skills throughout this process, otherwise the questions may become inquisitorial. Always paraphrase or reflect back what the service-user says in response to your question. This enables the person to appreciate fully what they have said.

ACTIVITY 6.3

Find someone to work with and ask them if you can practise future possibilities questions *on them. Explain the principles to them so they understand what they are agreeing to do with you. Now try the following:*

- *Ask the person the* magic wand question.

- *When the person responds, follow this with* and what would that do for you?

- *Use an empathic reflection to paraphrase what the person has inferred from their response.*

- *Discuss the activity with the speaker and ask for their feedback about this exercise.*

You can also try applying the *magic wand question* to yourself by doing the following exercise.

ACTIVITY 6.4

- *Ask yourself the* magic wand question.

- *Follow this up by asking yourself* and what would that do for me?

- *Write down your response.*

- *Assess what you have learned about what would help you with regard to future possibilities.*

COMMENT

When we first see the magic wand question it can appear to be a somewhat bizarre question to ask. This is why it is essential to follow up with and what would that do for you? Actually doing the above exercises can help you to see how useful this question is to have in your tool box of skills.

Using future possibility questions in challenging situations

Future possibility questions can also be used in more difficult and challenging situations where it might be tempting just to tell the service-user what to do. Below we explore some examples of this.

EXAMPLE 1

This example re-visits Donna (from Chapter 5) who has a four-year-old daughter Maddie and who is having a relationship with Eddie, who is on the Sex Offenders' Register. Let us assume that despite your best efforts at challenging Donna, she chooses to continue her relationship with Eddie. She knows you will arrange a case conference where legal advice will be sought to begin proceedings to protect Maddie. Donna is effectively choosing Eddie at the expense of her daughter. It would be tempting here for you as Donna's social worker to tell her to end her relationship with Eddie (thus taking control and removing the decision making from Donna). Instead, you could try helping Donna to project herself forward in time and explore future possibilities in the following way:

> Donna, I am wondering if you have really thought what your life might be like in the future if you continue your relationship with Eddie. I am asking you to think ahead to a year from now. Imagine you are living with Eddie. Maddie has been removed from your care and she is living with another family as their foster child. You are seeing her for an hour once a week in a community centre with a social worker present supervising the visit. What would this situation be like for you?

Asking Donna to imagine what her life might be like in the future acts as both a means of future projection and also a final challenge (although you would need to be careful not to use this as an opportunity to manipulate or threaten the service-user).

EXAMPLE 2

Here, we re-visit Jack and his five-year-old daughter Jenny, also from Chapter 5. Jenny has been sent home from school because she has scabies and on previous visits you have found Jack struggling to cope as a single parent. His house is very dirty and you are worried this will exacerbate Jenny's health problems. You could ask Jack the following future possibilities question:

Continued

EXAMPLE 2 *continued*

What would help you to manage a little better at home with Jenny?

Or

If you were managing a little better at home, what would need to be in place that is not there now?

The purpose of such questions is to help Jack start to think of ways forward which might help him:

> **Jack:** I think I need some help to get back on my feet. Admitting I am not coping is hard to do but there it is: I am not handling anything well at the moment. I am feeling so down. When I take Jenny to the doctor's I need to ask her if she could help me too. What would also help is a clean house – it is in such a state I don't know where to start.

> **You:** I know it feels like a big step but talking to your GP would be a very positive way forward. She will be able to help you to cope better. Getting on top of the house is really necessary and will also help you to cope with everything better. Do you have any ideas who might be able to help you with this?

Egan (2010, p305) writes that problems can make clients feel hemmed in and closed off. He goes on to say that the real power of helping is in assisting service-users to find their own solutions by setting and accomplishing goals. The above example demonstrates how Jack is likely to begin feeling better about himself once he sets and achieves some goals for himself.

EXAMPLE 3

Anne was also someone we met in Chapter 5. Anne is becoming increasingly afraid of her son Matt's behaviour. Last week, Matt assaulted her when she tried to get him out of bed to go to school. To help Anne improve her management of Matt's behaviour you could ask her to identify her most pressing needs:

> I know it has been very difficult for you because you are becoming increasingly frightened of Matt, especially since he hit you last week. What would help you most to get him out of bed and go to school in the mornings?

Or

> If things were working a little better in a morning, what would you be doing differently with Matt?

Or

> What would this situation look like if you were managing it a little better?

Rogers (1961) reminds us that the service-user is the expert on herself. In the above example, acknowledging that Anne knows herself better than anyone else and helping her to imagine what a different way of managing Matt would look like can help her to take control.

As noted previously, a big temptation when working with service-users, especially when they are in crisis, is to tell them what to do. Indeed, O'Sullivan (2011) comments that inexperienced social workers mistakenly believe their role is to solve problems rather than working with service-users to help them re-gain some control over their lives. Remembering to find out what people's most pressing needs are and to help them to imagine a different future assists service-users to develop a sense of direction for themselves. The service-user can then be helped to work out the detail of their preferred scenario and shape it into a specific goal (Wosket, 2006). Goal setting and accompanying strategies will be explored next.

Step 2B: Helping service-users to set effective goals

Once the service-user is able to see some possibilities for a better future, they can be helped to formulate some clear goals. Wosket (2006) suggests asking the service-user to identify what appeals to them most from their preferred scenarios. Service-users often need help in changing vague desires into concrete goals. For this process, Wosket suggests using the acronym SMART which she has adapted from Doran (1981):

Specific (not vague but concrete)

Measurable (verifiable, with a completion time or event)

Appropriate (will make a difference)

Realistic (achievable and within the person's capabilities at this time)

Timed (set within a reasonable time to complete).

Imagine we are going to use SMART targets in our work with Jack (from the example above). Jack has stated he knows he needs to have his house in a clean and manageable state. If his goal remains in this form, it will stay as a vague hope rather than a goal which is likely to come to fruition. If you were working with Jack you could guide him to develop his goal using questions relevant to each stage. For example, you might say to him the following:

You: *Your goal needs to be something concrete. How could you make it really specific so you would know exactly what it is you need to do?*

Jack: *I need to throw out the rubbish and do a proper spring clean, one room at a time, starting with the kitchen.*

You: *That sounds good. How will you know when you have reached your goal of a clean house?*

Jack: *Each room will look and smell clean. It will also look tidy.*

You: *You have a clear picture of what your house will look like after you have finished. If you achieve your goal and clean the house, what difference will this make to you?*

Jack: *I will feel I am taking better care of Jenny and I won't feel embarrassed about people coming into my house to visit me.*

You: *You have set yourself quite a challenging goal, how realistic do you think it is for you to do all of this on your own?*

Jack: *Mm. That's a good point. I'm not very good at cleaning and getting started is a problem for me because it is such a mess. If I just think about it as one room at once rather than a whole project I will feel more motivated.*

You: *Tackling it in smaller chunks makes it a more realistic goal. What sort of time frame do you think would be do-able for you? By what date would you be able to have finished the kitchen for instance?*

Jack: *Yes, having dates would help me to keep focused. The kitchen is the worst and realistically it will probably take me a week to get it sorted.*

Jack's goal is now to clean his house from top to bottom beginning with the kitchen, which he intends to complete by one week today.

Planning goals in this way makes it more likely they will be achieved. If any of the SMART elements do not stand up to scrutiny, the goal can be re-evaluated and changed to make it more robust. For example, if Jack had said he was working overtime for the next two days, he would have to consider whether or not he could do this in addition to cleaning the kitchen.

ACTIVITY *6.5*

Think about a goal you have set yourself recently.

- *Take the SMART criteria from above and apply each element to your goal.*

- *Assess whether or not your goal meets the criteria.*

- *Plan your final goal using SMART targets.*

COMMENT

Using the SMART criteria to re-evaluate your goal helps to make it as robust as possible. Once you have formed a well-crafted goal you are more likely to put it into practice.

Step 2C: Weighing up the costs and benefits of the goal

Once an effective goal has been set by the service-user, the next task of the practitioner is to help the service-user to assess their commitment to the goal. Egan (2010) suggests that helping service-users to choose goals which appeal to them is one way of helping them to become committed to action. The practitioner can also help the service-user to assess what might stop them from achieving the goal. One way of doing this is to help the person work out what they might have to give up if they wish to achieve the goal. In Chapter 5 we explored the case study of Karen, who is seeking help for drug dependency. Her goal is to stop taking drugs. However, the costs and consequences for herself in achieving this goal will be to lose some of her social contacts because she will need to avoid mixing with those of her friends who are drug users.

There are times when the service-user has little choice but to change their behaviour and achieve goals which are effectively set for them by their social worker. This is especially likely in cases of child protection, where there are legal requirements imposed. Jack, in his neglect towards Jenny, is a good example of a service-user in this situation. He is required to clean his house to an acceptable standard and to attend properly to Jenny's health-care, otherwise interventions will be sought. In cases where the goal is effectively being imposed by others, Egan (2010, p346) states that it is important to help the service-user to address *what am I doing to make it my own?* If you were working with Jack you would need to help him to own and take on this goal as something he wishes to achieve for himself. Jack clearly wants to continue to care for Jenny and so needs to make their home a safe environment for her.

Helping the service-user to explore the repercussions of their intended goal can help them to commit more fully. Woskett (2006, p81) states that we need to help the service-user to *weigh up the costs and consequences of pursuing goals.* With regard to Jack, if he spends a week cleaning the kitchen, a cost for him is refusing overtime at work. This may have financial consequences for him, which he will need to consider. If, however, he does not begin a cleaning regime, the consequences will be a greater involvement of statutory services. It is important not to resort to *'if you don't do x... then y will happen'.* A more positive way forward would be to help Jack to look at the benefits of beginning the cleaning. This is more likely to motivate him to carry on with his goal.

ACTIVITY **6.6**

Take the goal you set for yourself in activity 6.5. Assess your commitment to your goal by asking yourself some, or all, of the following questions:

- *What would I gain if I pursued this goal?*

- *What would help me to be more committed to the goal?*

- *What support would help me to stay committed?*

- *What are the costs involved for me in achieving my goal?*

- *What would be the consequences if I do achieve it?*

- *What would be the consequences if I do not achieve it?*

Finish the exercise by deciding whether or not your goal holds up to this level of scrutiny. If it does not, you will need to alter your goal.

COMMENT

Making space to reflect on goals should ensure that you maintain your commitment to the goal. It is also better to spend a little time on this now rather than progressing with a goal which is not robust and which will fail in the future. In the next section, we will explore developing strategies for achieving goals.

Egan model stage 3, helping service-users to develop plans and strategies for achieving goals

Once the service-user has developed a robust goal, the next step is to assist them to devise strategies that will help them both to achieve their goal and sustain subsequent change. Egan (2010) states that stage two of the helping process is about deciding outcomes and stage three consists of activities that enable the outcome to be met.

Step 3A: Identifying possible strategies

Achieving goals does not happen simply by wanting something to happen. According to Egan (2010), goals need to be underpinned by a set of workable strategies. These tactics will support the service-user throughout the process of change and will be especially helpful when progress is hard-going.

In keeping with other skills we have developed already, the more the service-user can be in control of this process, the more likely a successful outcome will be the result. Therefore, it is important that service-users are encouraged to devise their own strategies that will help them to achieve their goal. A good way to do this is to ask the service-user to think up as many strategies as possible which may help them to achieve their goal. The idea is to work quickly and for you to write down on a sheet of paper everything said, no matter how outlandish the idea seems. Egan encourages quantity rather than quality at this stage, and advises being mindful not to criticise any of the suggestions. If the service-user runs out of ideas, you as the helper can also add some suggestions to the sheet. Once the list is finished, read it back to the service-user and invite them to indicate which strategies appeal to them the most.

Imagine you are continuing to work with Jack:

> **You**: *What strategies can you think of that would help you to clean your kitchen next week?*
>
> **Jack**:
>
> - *If I could find someone to help me that would be great.*
>
> - *I could ask my sister.*
>
> - *I need to say no to my boss when he asks me to do overtime next week and then I will have more time.*
>
> - *I could get up a couple of hours earlier and do some before going to work.*
>
> - *I might be able to pay a professional firm to come in and do it if it is not too expensive.*
>
> **You**: (Sharing the sheet with Jack) *Which of these strategies appeals to you the most?*
>
> **Jack**: *I can't really afford to get a professional firm in. My sister has offered help in the past but I have felt too ashamed to take her up on it. I think this would be my best bet, I would feel awful asking her but I know she would help me out.*

You: *I can see it is going to be difficult for you to ask your sister but approaching her for help would be a very positive way forward. It sounds from what you have said that she already recognises you are struggling and she wants to get involved. It may make her feel good to know she is able to help you because she could be concerned about Jenny.*

The above example demonstrates that the service-user needs to be encouraged to choose a strategy that they feel is right for them.

Step 3B: Assessing the strategy

Once the service-user has chosen a strategy, the role of the practitioner is to help them to assess how effective it will be in achieving the goal. Wosket (2006, p89) suggests using the acronym CRAVE to see if the strategy fits the goal:

Control: *is this strategy in the client's control?*

Relevant: *does it address the goal?*

Appeal: *is it attractive to the client?*

Values: *is it in keeping with the client's values?*

Environment: *what external resources and constraints might help/hinder?*

In Jack's case, the strategy is within his control because he has a good relationship with his sister and although it is difficult for him, he is able to ask her for support. It is relevant because it will address the goal and is the most attractive option for Jack from his list. His values are that he wants and needs the house to be clean, even though it is currently in a dirty and dishevelled state. Finally, in terms of his environment, asking his sister to help will mean he is not paying large sums to an external organisation.

Step 3C: Formulating a plan

The final stage is to produce a formal plan. Wosket (2006) notes that sometimes the strategy chosen naturally forms a plan but at other times the service-user needs some help to think about the sequence of what needs to be done, together with a definite time frame.

We could work in the following way with Jack:

You: *What would help you make the first move to contact your sister?*

Jack: *I still feel so ashamed but I need to bite the bullet and go and see her. She lives about 15 minutes' walk away.*

You: *I know it is hard for you because you feel embarrassed but that sounds like a good plan. If it was the other way around and your sister was asking you for help, how would you feel?*

Jack: *I wouldn't think twice.*

You: *If she was in need, you would want to help as much as you could. When can you see her?*

Jack: *I will go round tonight and ask her if she can come round and help me tomorrow.*

You: *You have a definite strategy there which will really help your situation. Let's review how you get on with it when we meet next week.*

Good plans should be well designed and according to Egan (2010) should produce results. If the service-user places obstacles in the way then the impediments would need to be challenged. You could do this by using the challenging skills from Chapter 5. Helping the service-user to think of ways in which they can adhere to their strategy, including what they will do to overcome any obstacles, will help them to remain committed to the plan.

Egan states that using Lewin's *force field analysis* (Lewin, 1969, cited in Egan, 2010) can also help service-users to review their plans of action. Force field analysis consists of identifying the factors ('forces') which will get in the way of following the plan. It also involves listing facilitating factors which will help in implementing the plan. Planning to strengthen the factors that help and to dilute the factors that hinder will enable the service-user to anticipate difficulties along the way towards achieving the goal. This will place them in a better position to deal with obstacles as they arise. It will help also in weighing one set of factors in relation to the other – the 'pros and cons' – and thereby will serve to prevent service-users from becoming stuck.

ACTIVITY 6.7

Return to the goal which you set for yourself in activity 6.5 and for which you assessed your commitment in activity 6.6.

- *Write down all the strategies you can think of that might help you to achieve your goal.*

- *Choose a strategy that appeals to you.*

- *Apply the CRAVE criteria to your strategy to assess whether or not it will assist you fully in achieving your goal.*

- *Finally, write a plan which contains details of how you will carry out your strategy. Make sure you list a sequence of necessary actions by stating what you need to do first, second, third, etc.*

- *List the obstacles to your plan and state how you will overcome each of these.*

- *List the facilitating forces that will help you.*

- *Carry out your plan.*

- *Afterwards, review how successful the plan was in helping you to achieve your goal.*

COMMENT

The more appealing you can make the strategy and the more specific and watertight is the plan, the more likely you would be to achieve your goal. In social work practice, it would be important to follow up and review the plan in later sessions with service-users.

CHAPTER SUMMARY

If service-users are to be helped to manage their problems, then we need to work in partnership with them and help them to re-gain control over their lives. As practitioners we need to use skills which help service-users to identify effective solutions to difficulties for themselves. We need to recognise that service-users are the experts on their own problems and that we need to help each person to identify what would help them the most. It is important for us to continue using listening skills to establish what service-users need. We then need to encourage them to set their own specific and concrete goals because owned and well-crafted goals lead to clear solutions to difficulties.

Of course, not all needs and wishes can be fulfilled. Resources are often scarce and one of the roles of the practitioner is to assess the viability of service-users' goals. When goals prove not to be realistic, challenging skills developed in previous chapters can be used to help the service-user to re-frame them into something more achievable. Where goals are determined by statutory procedures (for example, in addressing neglect) helping the service-user to take ownership of the goal will become a priority for the practitioner.

Once owned and clear goals have been established, the service-user can be encouraged to devise and choose their own strategies. This process leaves people in control of their own lives and consequently more likely to achieve their goals. Learning how to devise clear goals and strategies gives service-users valuable skills that they can use in the future to help them self-manage challenging situations. Therefore, time spent helping service-users to better manage their current problems is a sound investment for their future.

FURTHER READING

Egan, G (2010) *The skilled helper: A problem management and opportunity development approach to helping*. 9th edition. Belmont CA: Brooks/Cole.

Two chapters are recommended: Chapter 11, Stage 2: The preferred picture – help clients design and commit to a better future; and Chapter 12, Stage 3: The way forward – help clients develop plans to accomplish goals. Both of these chapters offer detailed guidance on how to help service-users identify goals and accompanying strategies.

O'Sullivan, T (2011) *Decision making in social work*. 2nd edition. Basingstoke: Palgrave Macmillan.

This is a very interesting and readable book and, again, two chapters are recommended. First, Chapter 3, Involving service users and carers, discusses why it is important to involve service-users and carers and describes the various levels of involvement which can be achieved. Second, Chapter 7, Analysing options, explores risk in decision making and describes a helpful model which can assist practitioners and service-users to analyse available options.

Wosket, V (2006) *Egan's skilled helper model: Developments and applications in counselling*. Hove: Routledge.

Chapter 3, Overview of the skilled helper model 2: stages two and three, is a very effective summary of how the latter two stages of Egan's model can be used in practice.

Chapter 7
Working with loss and grief

Introduction

Loss is an important part of life and can have profound effects on life course development and mental and physical health. Experiencing loss in childhood can shape our attitudes and values and these in turn can influence how we cope with loss later in life. Grief can be defined as the way we respond to loss. These responses can be emotional (such as feeling and expressing sadness or anger), physical (for example, experiencing headaches or stomach problems) or behavioural (for example, not wanting to leave the house or see people). Thompson (2000) argues that much of social work is about working with service-users who are facing loss and that practitioners need to use counselling skills to help those who are grieving. We have already established that part of our role as practitioners is to try and understand service-users, and to do this well we need to develop awareness of where and how loss has affected their lives. Loss and its consequences can easily be overlooked in practice and it is important that we become mindful of this area if we are to become skilled practitioners.

This chapter will help you to recognise features of loss and grief and to understand how it affects people's lives. We will begin by defining loss and exploring why such an understanding is important in social work. The chapter will then explore different theories and models of loss. Working with people who are facing their own death is a highly challenging area of social work and we will explore ways of working with individuals and families experiencing life-limiting illnesses. Finally, there will be an exploration of further skills we can develop to help us to work with people experiencing loss and grief including working with children and older people.

How people experience loss

Loss and grief are most often associated with death. However, there are many other kinds of loss which bring about similarly strong levels of grief. In social work practice, loss is likely to feature as a defining element with many service-users.

Currer (2007) defines loss other than bereavement as secondary loss, although the person's reaction to this can be just as strong. Examples include loss of sight, or a limb; or when a child leaves home, or loss of a role in the workplace when we retire or are made redundant. Children may experience secondary loss when they are removed from their families and also perhaps when they leave a foster placement or residential home. Parents may experience loss if their child is removed from their care. Older people are also very likely to experience loss when they move from their own home into residential care. Such a change encompasses loss not only of their physical home but also of their neighbours, pets, independence and their sense of belonging. Bridges (1991) tells us that we need to recognise that change often involves loss. We need to identify particular changes which cause profound loss for service-users and help them to find ways of coping.

It is very important to continue to recognise something that we learned in an earlier chapter, i.e. that every person we are working with is an individual and, as such, will have their own unique way of responding to loss. Currer (2007) emphasises that not everyone experiences loss in the same way. For example, for one person, redundancy may be devastating, but for another it may be seen as an opportunity to do something different. For a great many people, the death of a partner may be the most difficult situation they have ever faced. However, for someone who has endured an unhappy relationship, the death of their partner might bring feelings of relief rather than sorrow. We need to be mindful to work in a non-judgemental way and to find ways of helping individuals to express their own responses (Egan, 1996).

We all have experience of loss and our own coping style can influence our expectations of others in a similar position (Currer, 2007). Until these unconscious processes become conscious, we are likely to lead and direct our service-users in the same way as we ourselves coped. For example, if my experience of coping with bereavement was to try to get back to normal as quickly as possible by returning to work immediately and avoiding talking about the person who died, then I am in danger of influencing the service-user into a similar course of action. Try the following activity to uncover your own patterns of responding to loss.

ACTIVITY 7.1

Think of a major loss or change which you have experienced in your life. This might involve the death of someone, or it could be a secondary loss such as moving house, school or job, or perhaps losing a favourite object.

- *How did you feel after your loss?*

- *How did you behave?*

Now think of someone else you know who has experienced a loss.

- *How did you expect the person to feel and behave?*

- *How different was their response from yours?*

COMMENT

We develop our own ways of managing loss and when we see someone else experiencing loss, it is easy to think we have the answers and a way forward for them. We need to recognise there are likely to be differences and that we are separate from the other person. Recognising differences is the first step in working effectively because in doing so we are much more likely to be able to help the service-user to tell us their story about their own loss, their reactions to it and consequently for us to hear fully what they are saying.

Later in this chapter we will explore ways of supporting service-users experiencing loss. Next, we will look at some of the ways in which practitioners fail to recognise grief in service-users.

RESEARCH SUMMARY

Currer (2007) in her research on loss found that social work students find it difficult to acknowledge and respond to the grief service-users display when talking about their losses. Currer comments that practitioners sometimes fail to engage because they worry about opening the floodgates, or feel they may do more harm than good. Other reasons include being reminded of their own losses, genuine pressure of work and worries about stepping on the toes of other workers.

Currer states that while some of the reasons may be legitimate, engaging at a deeper level by saying, for example, 'I can see this is very painful for you' may not be as time consuming and demanding as we think and is always better than ignoring the service-user's distress.

The skills of working with loss encompass everything you have learned previously in this book, especially empathic responding to help the person to tell their story when many people around them will not want to hear it because it is too painful. It is also helpful to have an understanding of various bereavement models and we shall briefly discuss some of these next.

Models for working with loss

There are various models that can help us to work with people who have experienced loss. While most models refer to bereavement, they can also be used to help people experiencing secondary loss. Early models tend to be a little prescriptive and imply that people progress through clearly defined stages, reaching a state of final acceptance. One such example is Kubler-Ross's (1973) five-stage model devised from her interviews with 200 patients facing their own death. She found the following coping mechanisms were often experienced: denial and isolation; anger; bargaining; depression; and acceptance. Her model helps to prepare practitioners in their support of dying service-users and has become widely used in this work, although Kastenbaum (2000) states that when people are facing their own death, responses are individual. Some people may display shock and distress whereas others may have a more philosophical attitude in addressing their own mortality.

Worden (1991) developed a helpful model, which describes tasks of mourning and has become a frequent way of working.

RESEARCH SUMMARY

Worden's tasks of mourning (developed in 1982 and refined in 1991)

Worden (1991, p34) describes mourning as the process which occurs after a loss while grief refers to the personal experience of the loss. Worden describes a range of ways in which grief may be manifested. These include: shock; anger; sadness; guilt; self-reproach; anxiety; loneliness; fatigue; helplessness; yearning; emancipation; relief; and numbness. He warns against using a 'stage' approach because of the danger of expecting certain types of behaviour. However, describing feelings and stages that the service-user might experience helps us to recognise them as a normal part of the grieving process.

The tasks with which the practitioner can assist the service-user are described as follows:

1. *Help the service-user to make the loss real by working through the strong emotions of denial and disbelief.*

2. *Provide time and space to grieve by helping the service-user to identify their feelings, allowing for individual differences.*

3. *Adjust to the loss by identifying coping strategies.*

4. *Help the service-user with the relocation of their loss by saying goodbye and feeling comfortable in moving on with their life. Here, instead of overwhelming the person, the loss becomes part of their life.*

5. *Identify where the service-user needs further help and refer them on if this is needed.*

Currer (2007, p55) reminds us that we *can't assume that grief is universal or follows the same pattern*. Currer also writes that the danger in having a model to follow can mean we dismiss the service-user's feelings because we see them as a 'stage'. It is very important, therefore, that we do not impose a model on the service-user. We need to take the same approach as we have throughout this book and see the other person as a unique individual who will act and react in their own way.

More recent grief-work models focus more specifically on individual differences. One example is Stroebe and Schut's (1999) *dual process model*.

RESEARCH SUMMARY

The dual process model.

Stroebe and Schut (1999) describe two aspects to bereavement: loss orientation *and* restoration orientation. *Loss orientation involves grieving and yearning and being pre-occupied with the loss event. Restoration orientation involves helping the service-user to cope with their new life and find a way forward by building a new identity. Stroebe and Schut state that it is important for the service-user to periodically take time off from the exhausting process of grieving, otherwise they will feel overwhelmed.*

Payne et al. (1999) comment that it is important to recognise that the service-user will oscillate between the two orientations described above. Currer (2007) comments that we need to remember this when making an assessment because there is a danger we could get a distorted view of the person's mental state. Payne et al. (1999) also add that individuals may favour one orientation over the other due to individual differences of culture and gender. For example, some male service-users may find it difficult to express feelings of grief but may be more able to engage in practical ways forward.

It is useful to remember that although both Worden, and Stroebe and Schut developed their models for helping people who are bereaved, we can also use the principles to help service-users who are experiencing secondary loss. We also need to be mindful that service-users have often experienced multiple losses and current losses can trigger feelings associated with earlier events.

Using the Egan model to help with loss

Tools we have already developed from Egan's Skilled Helper model sit clearly alongside both Worden's tasks of mourning and Stroebe and Schut's dual process model. Remember Egan advocates helping the person to tell their story. It is important to listen to the service-user's experience of loss by using empathic listening skills. This provides a safe space for the service-user to talk about their feelings freely, something they may not be able to get from people close to them. Gentle challenging, helping the service-user to recognise their strengths and to say what would help them to cope also echoes Egan, as does identifying strategies for coping. The dual process model emphasises the importance of enabling expression of feeling together with finding a way forward that meets the individual needs of the service-user.

In the following case study we will explore how a combination of the models described above could help you to work with an older service-user.

Malcolm

Malcolm is 75 years old and was married for 50 years to Dorothy, who died three months ago. He has recently moved from their marital home into sheltered accommodation. Malcolm and Dorothy had three children. Donald and Susan are in their forties, live in the next town and visit regularly. Malcolm and Dorothy's third child, Rebecca, died suddenly five years ago. You are visiting Malcolm on his return home from hospital after being admitted for observation after a fall. The hospital staff suspect Malcolm fainted due to lack of food. Dorothy provided all meals throughout their marriage and he is finding it hard to motivate himself to prepare food. Donald and Susan are worried about him because he is losing weight and they are now working in rotation to bring him a hot meal each day. During your visit Malcolm tells you how much he misses Dorothy. He doesn't like to talk to Donald and Susan about it because he wants them to think he is alright.

ACTIVITY *7.2*

Imagine you are working with Malcolm.

- *Identify the losses that Malcolm has experienced/is experiencing in his life.*

- *How might Worden's tasks of mourning help you to work with Malcolm?*

- *How might an understanding of the dual process model assist you?*

- *How would your knowledge of the Egan model help you?*

Working with Malcolm

Malcolm has suffered a number of major losses in his life. His daughter died suddenly and it is likely that he had to cope with not only his own feelings around this event but also those of Dorothy who may also have become 'lost' to him. He is also coping with the death of Dorothy and his old way of life, including the loss of their marital home. He is oscillating between loss and restoration (Stroebe and Schut), experiencing grief and also having to build a new identity by learning to look after himself and cope alone. Worden's and Egan's models help us to remember the importance of providing space and time to hear Malcolm's story, to engage with his grief and to help him find ways forward so he can develop strategies for managing his life without Dorothy. Our engagement with Malcolm could take place as follows:

Malcolm: *I still can't get used to her not being here.*

You: *You were together such a long time. I can see how much you miss Dorothy and how lost you feel without her.*

Malcolm: *I am not coping very well without her. I just sit here thinking about all the good times we had. And then I think about Rebecca too and what a blow her death was to Dorothy. She was never the same after that.*

> **You**: *I can't imagine how awful that must have been for you too. It must have been devastating for you not only to lose Rebecca but also to experience the profound effect it had on Dorothy.*

It is important to stay in the here and now with Malcolm and to use empathic responding skills to engage with him, even though this may be challenging for you. If Malcolm wants to talk about Dorothy and Rebecca, then stay with him in this process for as long as he needs to talk. When Malcolm is ready to begin looking ahead a little more, then take the opportunity to help him move forward:

> **Malcolm**: *Dorothy did all the cooking you know and I don't know where to start with doing it. Donald and Susan have been very good to me but I can't keep expecting them to bring me my meals.*

> **You**: *I know you miss Dorothy's cooking – and it must be so hard to find the energy and motivation to learn how to prepare meals for yourself. What would help you to manage a little better with your meals?*

Malcolm switches from loss orientation to restoration orientation when he begins expressing his worries about preparing food. At this point, using skills from stage two of the Egan (2010) model (finding out what the person wants or needs) helps us to assist Malcolm in exploring a better future.

Loss and anger

An intense emotion that is often experienced during the grieving process is anger and such feelings often take both the service-user and practitioner by surprise. Anger arises from the frustration of feeling helpless and is often displaced on to a recipient who has little to do with the original loss (Worden, 1991). Scrutton (1996) describes an incident where a new resident in an older persons' care home kicked a member of staff who was taking her to the toilet. The carer failed to recognise the indignity the service-user felt in requiring assistance for this most private of functions. Nor did she understand that the resident was angry and grieving for her loss of independence. We need to be mindful of Bridges' (1991) comment that change usually involves loss and that the grieving process resulting from loss often includes anger (Worden, 1991). Anger is often a dominant emotion in service-users who are facing life-limiting illnesses and we will explore this area next.

Working with service-users who have life-limiting illnesses

Although work in this area might be seen as specialist and the remit of hospice social workers, helping people who are facing their own death is likely to be part of your experience in other settings too. For example, you might find yourself working with a single parent who has recently received a diagnosis of cancer and who is worried about how her children will be cared for if and when anything happens to her. In a variety of settings you may also work with older people who are dying.

To identify particular skills which help practitioners to work with people who are dying and their families, I interviewed Mary who worked for many years as a hospice social worker.

Mary: Much of my work at the hospice involved working with single parents who had life-threatening illnesses, and their children. One of the most important aspects of social work in this area is helping people to make plans when others around them don't want to hear. It does help to have a model because it is useful to know what might happen, for example, the service-user might be angry with you but you know from the model that this is often displaced anger.

I found anger harder to work with than the sadness, but you need to acknowledge it and use your Egan skills to do this – gentle challenging skills are often the only way forward. You need to get in there and investigate what the anger is about and help them recognise it if that is appropriate. There are two levels to anger – dealing with emotions and then thinking where does that come from because emotions can have profound effects on families. If anger is directed at you, then that's better than when it is towards a family member. Anger is most difficult to work with when the service-user directs it at themselves, for example when someone self harms as a reaction, say, to not being able to keep their son alive.

I don't like it when someone is described as being 'stuck' in a stage of grief. For me, it's a time when there aren't any rules – anything goes. Egan's model has been the most useful model for me – using active listening because people have a very individual way of expressing loss. Your role is to try and help them to make sense of all the confusing feelings they are having. Your non-judgemental skills are tested the most and you need to constantly look at your own values and not impose them. It is also important to recognise the intensity of the service-user's feelings – and this is not often written about – the overwhelming feelings people have because they have no coping strategies. You need to be able to acknowledge people feel helpless and to cope with feeling helpless yourself – tears from the helper are OK although of course it is not alright to be distraught.

Once families start to look forward then this is the time to withdraw. You need to acknowledge you are not always useful and you need to question why you are there because your work can slip into a comfy chat if you are not careful. You also need to manage endings effectively because this can become another loss for the service-user. It is also important to identify abnormal grief and recognise when your role has ended and someone else needs to get involved.

It is clear from Mary's comments that she has found Egan's Skilled Helper model very useful in her work because it offers a framework of empathic responding, gentle challenging and future planning. In the next section we will consider another important point made by Mary, the need to recognise when to refer the service-user for more specialist help, for example from a mental health practitioner.

Recognising the need for referral

It is essential that we are able to recognise signs and symptoms which indicate the service-user requires more specialised help than we can offer. Worden (1991) comments that clinical depression can be a complication that develops after a loss. He states that it occurs when normal feelings of depression following a loss expand into irrational despair and total hopelessness. Suicidal feelings, panic attacks and phobias can signal that the service-user is clinically depressed and may be in need of referral. If any of these issues are raised, (particularly thoughts of suicide), it is important that you seek immediate guidance from your supervisor.

Some people experience Post Traumatic Stress Disorder (PTSD), which may consist of sudden outbursts of anger, acute anxiety and recurrent and intrusive recollections of the loss (Scott and Stradling, 2006). Maintaining the welfare of service-users is of paramount importance (Connor, 1994) and supervision is a vital vehicle for identifying our limitations and exploring circumstances requiring referral (Hawkins and Shohet, 2007).

In the final section of this chapter we will use a case-study approach to explore ways of working with service-users and their families who are experiencing loss and grief.

Working with children who are experiencing loss and grief

Working with bereaved children can be an emotionally challenging task for social work practitioners. *Winston's Wish* is an organisation that supports bereaved children. It emphasises that the death of a parent is one of the most difficult losses a child will ever face and that their response will vary according to their previous experience of loss, how the parent died and the child's age.

Dyregrov (1991) states that a child under the age of five does not understand the finality of death and that we should be careful of the terminology we use when working with them. Phrases such as *Grandma has gone to sleep* or *we have lost Mum* are likely to be taken literally with the child thinking Grandma will wake up or Mum will be found. In the age-range from five to ten children gradually realise that death is final and can understand some of the reasons why people die. They are more likely to believe the dead person can see or hear them and may consequently work hard to please them (Dyregrov, 1991). Between the age of ten and adolescence the child is more able to understand the facts involved with the death and to reflect on the long-term consequences. They may fear the death of living people and also contemplate their own death. Loss experienced by adolescents brings further special difficulties. Currer (2007) states that a major feature of adolescence is the development of independence from parents and that this is difficult to manage when a parent dies.

When working with children it is important to appreciate that reactions to loss can take many forms. Dyregrov (1991) comments some children might display apathy and regression while others seem to continue as if nothing has happened.

Abrams (1999) cites Rosenman et al.'s (1994) study of 255 bereaved children. This study found children feel emotionally alone when a parent dies and very few have an adult to whom they can talk about their loss. The most common response was withdrawal and silence and half the children developed emotional problems in the first year after a parent's death. Abrams states that children hide their own distress because they feel protective towards the surviving parent and siblings. She also comments that although teachers often feel that a 'business as usual' approach to a child is best, this can cause the child to feel anxious because of the pressure to act normally and because they feel there is nowhere to turn if they are unable to cope.

Creative helping skills

Children and young people do not always have the language skills to express how they are feeling. Seeking out more creative ways of helping them is often useful. For example, with younger children, you could invite them to draw a picture of their life before the loss and another depicting life now. Asking the child to explain what is going on in the picture can be a way to better understand how they are feeling.

Another tool is to construct a genogram (McGoldrick et al., 2008). Genograms resemble a family tree and contain additional information indicating how family members and others relate to each other by using particular symbols. Both the construction of a genogram and art work are powerful methods of helping young people to tell their story and convey what is really going on for them. Then you can help the service-user to gain more control by finding out what would help them.

Next, we will consider how we might work with Danny who features in the following case study.

CASE STUDY

Danny

Danny is 17 years old and a full-time student at his local college studying carpentry and joinery. He is an only child and was brought up in a single-parent household until his mother died of breast cancer when he was 12. He has never known his father. On the death of his mother he moved 30 miles away to live with his grandmother, Agnes. During the last two years, Agnes developed heart problems and she became increasingly reliant on Danny to look after her. When Danny tried to wake Agnes on Monday morning, he discovered she had died in her sleep. When you visit, you find Danny distressed and worried about where he is going to live and how he will continue at college.

ACTIVITY 7.3

Imagine you are the practitioner visiting Danny.

- *Identify the losses Danny has experienced in his life.*

- *How would you respond to Danny's distress?*

- *How might various loss and grief models help you to understand what may be happening to Danny?*

- *How might Egan's Skilled Helper model help you to work with Danny?*

Working with Danny

Danny has already experienced multiple losses even before his grandmother died. He has had to cope with the death of his mother, which brought about other losses: he moved home and school and may have lost old school friends. He is also likely to have felt the loss of a relationship with his father. He has experienced the loss of leaving his new school when he started college. The death of his grandmother is the latest in a series of major losses for him, and he may also feel the loss of his role as a carer. Although it is important not to make any pre-judgements of Danny, models of loss might help us to recognise that Danny may be feeling shock, in particular because he discovered his grandmother's body. We know he is feeling sad, but we might also anticipate Danny feeling guilty in some way, numb and helpless. He seems to be oscillating between the pain of his loss and worrying about his future. It is important that we work alongside Danny without making any assumptions about how he expresses himself.

Being mindful of Egan's three-stage model (2010), if Danny wants to talk about his grandmother (and/or his other losses) then we need to use our stage one empathic listening skills to provide him with space to tell his story, but we should not force him to do this if he does not want to. Indeed, he is clearly telling us his needs, (relevant to stage two of Egan's model: identifying a better future), which are somewhere to live and a way of continuing with his college course. Using stage three skills of devising strategies for both finding a new home for Danny and ensuring his continuation at college can assist us in supporting him.

Working with loss: Older people entering residential care

Finally, in this chapter, we will explore some of the profound losses older people can experience when they enter residential care. As you read the following case study, try and place yourself in the shoes of Beatty to better understand the losses she experiences as an older person.

CASE STUDY

Beatty

Beatty is 77 years old and was widowed 20 years ago. She has recently entered residential care after suffering a stroke, which resulted in some paralysis of her right arm, leg and face. She understands others perfectly well but her own speech is slow as a result of the stroke. Beatty now needs help washing and dressing, getting up, going to bed and going to the toilet. Until her stroke, she was very independent, living in her own house. She saw her sister most days, with whom she had a good social life visiting friends and going on bus trips to various towns and villages. Her main passions were gardening and cooking. Beatty has a son and two grandchildren who live abroad and visit once a year. When you visit, Beatty's key worker tells you Beatty was verbally abusive towards her yesterday when she tried to coax her into the dining room for her lunch.

Continued

CASE STUDY *continued*

You recognise that Beatty has suffered a number of profound losses including her home, her health, independence and social contacts. Beatty is no longer in control of when and how she sees her sister. She has lost her house and beloved garden and the sense of well-being these gave her. She is no longer able to take a bus and go out for the day. She has lost her dignity in requiring help with dressing and toileting. She has also lost control of cooking her own meals, something she loved doing. Parts of Beatty's face and body are paralysed, including her right hand and these losses alone are likely to be leaving her utterly frustrated. She may also be grieving for the changes in physical appearance and may not want others to see her in the dining room: a public place. Her anger, directed at the key worker who meant well, is therefore understandable.

Working with Beatty would first require us to empathise with her losses by saying something like the following:

> Beatty, arriving here must have come as such a shock to you. I can imagine you are still absolutely reeling from everything that has happened. It must have been so hard to lose your home, your garden and everything that was familiar to you. And I can see how difficult it is for you to face other people at the moment because you are so upset about the changes in your body.

Using empathic responses can help Beatty to feel she can tell you what is happening to her. Later in the process, when Beatty is ready, you will be able to help her to cope better with her changed circumstances by establishing her new needs and wants.

CHAPTER SUMMARY

Whenever you are working with service-users experiencing change (which will be most of the time), my suggestion is to ask yourself two questions: *what losses might the person be experiencing and how are they grieving?* The sorrow and anger that result from loss and grief can cause great pain to both the service-user and their family. Learning to recognise some of the signs of loss and assisting the service-user to both express what is going on for them and to find ways forward can help them to move on with their lives. The listening, empathy and problem management skills you have learnt previously will help you in this process. Many social workers feel they do not have the skills for listening to feelings about loss and may wish to refer to another agency. This will often not be necessary. Having the confidence to use counselling skills and listening carefully enough to be led by the service-user will usually be sufficient. We need to help the person, when they are ready, to look ahead and plan their future, no matter how much or little time they have left. In so doing, we are placing service-users in control of their own lives.

Cruse Bereavement Care [Online]. Richmond. Available from: www.bereavementcare.org.uk

Cruse's website contains a wealth of material on bereavement including helping young people, traumatic losses and coping with crisis.

Currer, C (2007) *Loss and social work*. Exeter: Learning Matters.

This is a relevant, readable and up-to-date text for social work practitioners working with loss. Chapters 3 and 4 are particularly recommended.

Kubler-Ross, E (1973) *On death and dying*. London: Routledge.

The author writes about her own experience of working with people facing life-threatening illnesses and her work describes her own five-stage model on pp34–121.

Stroebe, M and Schut, H (1999) The dual process model of coping with bereavement: rationale and description. *Death Studies*, 23 (3): 197–224.

This journal article describes the authors' own model. It argues against a staged approach to loss and incorporates working with culture and gender.

Winston's Wish [Online]. Cheltenham. Available from: www.winstonswish.org.uk

This organisation provides information and practical support for families and professionals who are involved with bereaved children. A number of detailed help-sheets are available to download from their website.

Worden, JW (1991) *Grief counselling and grief therapy: A handbook for the mental health practitioner*. 2nd edition. London: Routledge.

The whole text is informative and thought provoking. However, in particular, Chapter 3 specifies Worden's *tasks of mourning* and Chapter 4 details abnormal grief reactions.

Chapter 8
Working with conflict

This chapter will help you to develop the following capabilities, to the appropriate level, from the **Professional Capabilities Framework**.

- **Professionalism**. Identify and behave as a professional social worker, committed to professional development.
- **Values and ethics**. Apply social work ethical principles and values to guide professional practice.
- **Knowledge**. Apply knowledge of human growth and development, psychological, social sciences, law and social work practice theory.
- **Critical reflection and analysis**. Apply critical reflection and analysis to inform and provide a rationale for professional decision-making.
- **Intervention and skills**. Use judgement and authority to intervene with individuals, families and communities to promote independence, provide support and prevent harm, neglect and abuse.

See Appendix 1 for the Professional Capabilities Framework diagram.

The chapter will also introduce you to the following standards as set out in the 2008 social work benchmark statement.

5.1.4 Social work theory.
5.1.5 The nature of social work practice.
5.5.3 Analysis and synthesis.
5.5.4 Intervention and evaluation.
5.6 Communication skills.
5.7 Skills in working with others.
5.8 Skills in personal and professional development.

Introduction

Anger, frustration and desperation are common emotions experienced by service-users and are regularly directed at practitioners. Being on the receiving end of someone else's vitriol can be at best disconcerting and at worst dangerous and we need to be vigilant to our own safety. Of course, if we feel in any way at risk from someone else's behaviour we need to prioritise protecting ourselves. Sometimes, the service-user's anger can be directed at someone else in the household. In these instances it is also best for us to remove ourselves and then seek immediate help for the vulnerable person. However, many conflict situations can be managed by using particular skills which we will explore in this chapter. Skills of empathic responding, Transactional Analysis and assertiveness will be further explored and applied in case study examples. We will also examine skills for conveying difficult information to people, including managing endings of social work relationships.

Keeping ourselves safe

Social work often involves working with people who are angry, upset and in crisis. In the previous chapter we explored how loss may produce feelings of anger and how violence and anger can be directed at practitioners. While there are never excuses for violence towards professional workers, reasons for anger can often be identified. The young person who enters residential care because his parent has chosen to live with a sex offender; the person being sectioned during an acute and terrifying psychotic episode; the mother whose new baby is being removed because she has a history of neglecting other children; the older person who has dementia and hits out in fear and frustration. All of these situations, and many more, can be predictable triggers to anger and violence.

In a special report for *Community Care Magazine* in 2010, McGregor found that nine out of ten social workers have suffered threats or assault, and councils in England recorded more than 45 000 violent incidents involving social care workers between 2007 and 2010. Lombard (2010) also found that on average, three social workers are assaulted each day. These statistics highlight the dangers practitioners can face on a daily basis.

Social workers need to be able to recognise when they are in danger and to know how to keep themselves safe. Mantell (2009) states that if we believe we are in danger of being assaulted, we need to withdraw immediately. Taylor (2011) advises us to hone our danger awareness in a number of areas. First, we need to do our homework before a first visit and find out whether a service-user has a history of violence. We also need to be vigilant for clues to a possible assault, for example is the service-user tense, invading our body space, clenching their fist, etc? Second, we need to be mindful of our task: are we, for example, bringing bad news? Third, we must consider the environment, for example, might other family members harm us? What objects could be used as weapons and how might we escape if we need to? Where should we sit, which is not confrontational for the service-user but equally enables a swift exit for us if need be? Fourth, Mantell tells us to be constantly aware of our own reactions and feelings to unfolding events. If we feel uncomfortable and threatened, then we need to recognise these feelings and be ready to leave the situation if necessary.

Having a high level of self-knowledge is important in assessing risk to ourselves. We need to understand our own personal responses to anger and how we transfer these onto the service-user. For example, if I am the sort of person who becomes afraid if someone raises their voice to me in any situation, I am likely to judge a service-user as being harmful to me and remove myself when this is not necessary. Equally, if I have grown up in an environment where raised voices, arguments and anger are normal events to me, I might not recognise the significance of a service-user who is escalating in their level of aggression towards me. We explored transference, or responding to service-users as we have previously responded to significant other people in our lives, in Chapter 4, and this knowledge will help us in this chapter.

Think of a recent incident when someone became angry with you.

- *How did you feel?*

- *How did you react?*

- *Are there any similarities between the above and how you felt and reacted as a child when your parent or caregiver was angry with you?*

- *How might you react if a service-user became angry with you?*

COMMENT

Our own pattern of responding when people are angry with us is likely to be unconscious until we think about it. Once we become aware of how we have learned to respond, we will be better able to consider each incident of anger on its own merits.

When a service-user's anger escalates into aggression and we feel ourselves or another person in the household to be in danger, then removing ourselves and seeking help is the best course of action. We always need to be mindful of risk and of the need to protect ourselves. However, there are many situations where service-users will feel angry and project that anger onto us without it escalating into an event which is dangerous for us. In these situations, there is a great deal we can do to work with and defuse people's anger. In the remaining sections of this chapter, we will explore skills that you can use in these scenarios. First, we will explore how we can convey information that the service-user might not want to hear.

Breaking bad news

One of the more challenging aspects of working with service-users is when we have to tell them news that will be difficult for them to accept. Examples include the following:

- Telling a young person in the looked-after system that they cannot return home.

- Informing parents that you are unable to procure the care they are seeking for their child who has a disability.

- Telling a parent that their child is being removed into local authority care.

- Informing a parent that their child is going to be adopted by another family.

- Explaining to an older person, who is being looked after by their partner, that their partner is now too ill and exhausted to continue caring for them and that alternatives need to be sought.

- Telling a young person in residential care that a family member has died.

Breaking bad news is never easy and requires a high level of interpersonal engagement. The skills you have already learned in this book, such as empathic responding and working with loss are essential and we will build on these here. Much of the guidance on communicating bad news is designed to help medical practitioners to convey diagnoses to patients but the same principles are also helpful for social workers.

Faulkner (1998) suggests that, ideally, the person breaking the news should be someone with whom the recipient feels comfortable. Having a good working relationship with the service-user can therefore be enormously helpful. The following strategy is a combination of suggestions from Faulkner (1998) and The National Council for Hospice and Specialist Palliative Care Services (2003). Let us imagine we are telling a young person, Kayleigh who is 12 and in residential care, that she cannot return home. Kayleigh's mother (a single parent) suffers from clinical depression, which is exacerbated by her use of drugs and alcohol.

Prepare yourself

Rehearse the meeting to yourself or with a colleague beforehand including thinking of questions the service-user is likely to ask you.

Prepare your setting

Make sure you are sitting at the same level as the service-user with no barriers. Make sure your mobile phone is switched off to avoid interruptions.

Identify current knowledge

Find out what the service-user knows or suspects. Often, the person will suspect bad news is coming.

> **You**: *These last few weeks must have been really hard for you. What are you making of it all?*

> **Kayleigh**: *I know my mum isn't coping, and I think she has got worse since I came in here. It's better if I can be at home to look after her.*

> **You**: *You know she is very unwell and not able to look after you.*

Prepare the ground

It is important to prepare the person for bad news, especially if they have little idea of what to expect. Even if the service-user does suspect, a warning statement helps them to make the leap to the news itself.

> **You**: *I've come straight from the court hearing: your case was heard this morning.*

> **Kayleigh**: *A decision has been made about what will happen to me?*

> **You**: *Yes, it has. I'm afraid the news is not what you were hoping to hear.*

Provide information at the service-user's pace and allow for shock

It is important to use vocabulary the person understands and not to rush them. Be clear and succinct and be careful not to overload the person. It is important to go at the recipient's pace because they are likely to be in shock upon hearing the news. Shock often means they then will not hear detailed or crucial information that follows, so wait before offering more information. Be sure to allow space for the person to take in the news.

> **You**: *Kayleigh, I know this is going to be very difficult for you to accept, but I have to tell you that you are not able to go home. You will stay here until we can find a suitable foster placement for you.*
>
> *There is silence for a while, during which you, also, say nothing. You maintain eye contact with Kayleigh to let her know you are with her, and you wait for her to respond.*
>
> **Kayleigh**: *(Crying) I can't believe it. I know she is in a bad way but we've always managed. All I've wanted is to go home. Does this mean I won't see her at all?*

Allow the service-user to choose when they have heard enough

Provide information as the service-user asks for it, but check out whether she would like further information later, when the shock has subsided, to discuss the facts more fully.

> **You**: *I know what a wrench it has been for you not to be at home looking after your mum and how much you miss her. Of course you will still be able to see her. We could talk about this now, or we could come back to how this will work another time.*
>
> **Kayleigh**: *As long as I can still see her. I can't believe I'm not going home.*

Kayleigh signals she is not able to discuss it now. It is important to allow the person to choose when they have heard enough.

Handle reactions and provide continuing support

It is important to acknowledge and stay with the emotions which are being expressed by the service-user, even if they leave you feeling uncomfortable. Focusing on difficult feelings can help the person to work through them.

> **Kayleigh**: *Why won't you let me go home? Something really bad will happen to her if I'm not there, I know it will and it will be your fault. You're all the same, you just don't understand. Why didn't you tell the judge that I need to go home?*
>
> **You**: *I know this is really difficult for you. You are desperately worried about your mum and feel angry because no one seems to be hearing how much you feel responsible for her.*
>
> **Kayleigh**: *I'm scared.*
>
> **You**: *I can see how frightened you are for her safety, and I want you to know I am here to help you.*

Provide a plan

The service-user is unlikely to be able to engage in a detailed plan at this stage. However, planning future support will help the person to feel more in control. With Kayleigh, it is important for her to know you will see her again soon.

> **You**: *I know the news today has been a shock to you and that you are going to need a little time to take it all in. How about we meet again tomorrow and plan together how you will stay in touch with your mum?*

Remember, even when we are breaking bad news, our aim is to continue placing the service-user at the centre of decision making. Working to a structure such as the one described above can help the service-user to remain in as much control as possible when they are receiving bad news. Empathic responding is very important here and needs to be present at every step of the process, even when the person's anger is directed towards us.

In this section, we have introduced the skill of using empathic responding to work with service-users who are expressing anger in the context of receiving bad news. In the next section, we will explore further techniques for working with service-users who are angry and potentially aggressive.

Using empathy together with placing the service-user at the centre of the process

At the beginning of this chapter it was made clear that if you are working with a service-user and feel yourself to be in danger, then you must leave the situation as soon as possible. However, you are likely to experience anger and conflict from service-users relatively regularly and the majority of these instances will not require you to beat a hasty retreat. Taylor (2011) suggests that the earlier you can detect anger and aggression, the more options you will have for defusing and resolving it. Rew and Ferns (2005) suggest that first of all we need to understand our own communication style and how this might impact on the service-user. Second, they recommend that we learn to understand and anticipate factors which trigger aggression, and suggest that a key trigger is when the service-user is not in control of a situation. Third, they advocate using therapeutic communication skills, such as empathy, stating that when we are working with someone who is angry, we need to put ourselves in their shoes to gain a better understanding of why they might be feeling this way.

Skills for working with conflict then, involve techniques which are already in our toolbox: self awareness; empathy; and placing the service-user in control. We will spend the rest of the chapter exploring how to use these familiar skills in conflict situations.

Earlier, we explored our responses to when someone becomes angry with us. Understanding how we may unwittingly exacerbate a tense situation is essential. Transactional Analysis (Berne, 1971) is a theory which we have already explored in Chapter 4 and which we can use here to analyse our own responses in conflict situations. Maintaining an Adult ego-state can help us to stay calm in conflict and it can also invite the service-user to change their ego-state into the Adult too. Remember, being in the Adult ego-state involves using empathy to try and understand what is happening to the service-user. It also involves respecting the service-user and ensuring they keep as much control as possible.

In the next case study, we will explore using Transactional Analysis, empathy and keeping the service-user in control in more detail.

CASE STUDY

Winnie is a 35-year-old single parent who has a 13-year-old daughter, Billie. A neighbour has reported hearing an altercation between them both and seeing Billie the following day with a black eye. Ken, a newly qualified social worker, visits Winnie and Billie at their home to carry out an assessment. When Winnie opens the door it is clear she is far from happy about the visit. The following dialogue takes place:

Winnie: I can't believe all this. Who reported me? Was it that interfering ***** from next door? Well was it? Tell me! (*Controlling Parent.*)

Ken: I can't tell you who reported you. The main thing is Billie has a black eye and we need to get to the bottom of it. (*Controlling Parent.*)

Winnie: Are you saying I did it? You are, aren't you! You are standing there, judging me when you haven't got the first idea about my life! (*Free Child.*)

Ken: I'm here to do an assessment. Where is Billie? I need to see her. (*Controlling Parent.*)

Winnie: Oh that's brilliant. You'll take one look at her and then you'll blame me. No, I'm not fetching her. You can't tell me what to do in my own home. (*Free Child.*)

Ken: Well, actually I can. Where's Billie? (*Controlling Parent.*)

Winnie: (*Threatening now*) Get out of my house!

In this scenario, Ken adopts an officious approach, relying increasingly on his Controlling Parent ego-state thinking this will give him control of the situation. He does this unconsciously in response to Winnie's own Controlling Parent and Free Child ego-states. Winnie is already angry and upset when Ken arrives and Ken's interpersonal style exacerbates Winnie's anger into full-blown aggression.

To manage the interaction better, Ken needs to use his Adult ego-state and invite Winnie to do the same:

Winnie: I can't believe all this. Who reported me? Was it that interfering ***** from next door? Well was it? Tell me! (*Controlling Parent.*)

Ken: Winnie, I can see you feel really angry that someone has called us, especially when you don't know who it was. I think if it was me getting an uninvited visit, I might also be feeling scared about what might happen. (*Adult – using empathy.*)

Continued

CASE STUDY continued

Winnie: I am scared. I can't tell you how humiliating it is to have you come round. Are you here to take Billie away? (*Adapted Child.*) There's no way I would let you do that. (*Free Child.*)

Ken: You and Billie sound really close. You're her mum and you don't want anything to come between you: you would fight for her all the way. (*Adult – using empathy.*)

Winnie: (Calmer) I love her so much. I'm so scared you are going to think I did it when you see her. (*Conveying feelings from her Adult ego-state.*)

Ken: You're afraid that I'm going to put two and two together and make five. Winnie, would you like to tell me what happened? (*Adult ego-state, empathic response and keeping the control with Winnie.*)

Winnie: OK. (*Adult.*)

In the second example, Ken maintains Adult responses throughout the interaction and does not become either defensive or controlling at any point. Using empathic Adult responses helps Winnie to feel heard and understood. By recognising her anger and fear, Ken defuses Winnie's aggression and the situation de-escalates. By using his Adult ego-state, Ken invites Winnie to communicate with him using hers too.

ACTIVITY 8.2

Think again of the incident you explored in activity 8.1 when someone became angry with you. Write down what the other person said to you and also how you responded.

- *Which ego-state did the other person use?*

- *Which ego-state did you use to respond?*

- *How could you have communicated from your Adult ego-state?*

COMMENT

When feelings are running high it is easy to slip into Parent and Child ego-state responses. This type of complementary transaction keeps both parties firmly entrenched in their own positions and the result can be an escalation of anger. Taking a step back and thinking of Adult responses is more challenging but can also be more fruitful.

Using assertiveness skills

The term *assertive behaviour* is often misunderstood. People often confuse assertiveness with aggression and think that being assertive means getting our own way. If we enter situations with such a win/lose mentality then we are making conflict much more likely (Dickson, 1982). We have already seen in the previous case study that once the service-user feels powerless, they can then experience fear. It is a short step from feeling fear to becoming aggressive.

Being assertive begins with respecting both ourselves and the service-user equally. Harris (1973, p49) describes this state as being *I'm OK and you're OK*. This means I respect, accept and feel confident about myself and I respect and accept you as a unique and autonomous human being. Believing the service-user is OK does not mean we have to like or agree with their behaviour or actions, but it does mean accepting them as a person in their own right. For example, if the service-user does something that we find unacceptable, then it is their action that we do not like rather than their whole being. This is an important distinction and one which can help us to keep respect at the heart of our practice.

Respect needs to be one of the basic underpinnings of engagement rather than being seen as a technique to draw on as required. If respect is fundamental to the way we are, then assertive communication will follow on more naturally.

Assertive behaviour means being open, honest, clear and specific in our communication. It also involves using negotiating skills and being willing to seek a compromise wherever this is possible. Our choice of language is also important. Using terms beginning with the word *you*, such as *you should...* or *you shouldn't...* or *you ought to...* or *why can't you just...* are aggressive rather than assertive statements. In Transactional Analysis terms, these phrases all arise from our Controlling Parent ego-state. Assertive communication, however, usually involves using *I* or *we* or *let us* statements such as *I know you feel very upset about... let's sit down and talk about it* rather than *you shouldn't get so upset about it* or *there's no need to take that tone*.

Being assertive means we should never put the other person down (McBride, 1998). Neither should we be passive. Passive behaviour includes saying *I'm sorry* when we have no need to apologise, failing to give eye contact, continually blaming ourselves and seeing ourselves as victims. McBride states that assertiveness includes being clear about our boundaries, being able to say *no* clearly and compassionately, giving criticism constructively, listening to criticism from others, and expressing anger without losing our temper. Keeping calm, using active listening and being empathic are all key components of being assertive.

ACTIVITY *8.3*

How assertive are you? Tick a), b) or c) in the following conflict scenarios.

1. *For the third time in a row, a parent is late for supervised contact with her son, Ryan.*

How would you respond?

   a) *I can't believe you are late again. It's not fair on Ryan you know.*

   b) *Not say anything.*

   c) *I can see it is difficult for you to make it to the sessions on time. I'm very conscious that Ryan is upset because he thinks you are not going to come. What can we do to address this?*

2. *Moira is adamant that her mother, Violet, needs to enter residential care. Violet wishes to stay in her own home.*

Continued

ACTIVITY *8.3 continued*

How would you respond?

a) *You're not listening to what your mum wants. You shouldn't be telling her what to do.*

b) *Yes, your mum really needs to see sense.*

c) *I know you are really worried and want what is best for her. But I am also hearing your mum say clearly that she does not want to go into a home. We need to find a way forward which is respectful to Violet's wishes and which also allays your fears.*

COMMENT

In each scenario, answers a) use a more aggressive response, answers b) are more passive and answers c) use assertiveness skills. The assertive responses are respectful of all parties, use empathy and also place each person as much as possible in control. In the next section we will explore assertiveness skills further.

Broken record

The broken record technique mirrors what happens to a vinyl record when the needle gets stuck, namely the repeating of a portion of the track (I appreciate that those of you born after 1980 might not know what I am talking about!). This assertiveness technique involves you repeating your message to the recipient until it has been heard. McBride (1998) describes this as being useful when your message is being deflected or ignored. Combined with empathy, the broken record technique can be useful in defusing angry situations. This is demonstrated in the following scenario. Imagine you visit a parent, Peter, who is angry because he feels that insufficient respite has been arranged for his daughter, Sian, 13, who has learning difficulties.

Peter: (Paces up and down with clenched fists). *We just can't cope. One weekend a month isn't enough. You've no idea what it's like. Sian doesn't sleep, and my wife and I are up, night after night. I'm so tired I don't know what I'm doing.*

You: *Peter, you are clearly at your wits' end* (empathic response). *Come and sit down with me and we'll talk about it.*

Peter: (Still pacing). *I am at my wits' end! And I'm going to lose my job if I can't get some proper sleep.*

You: *It must be awful for you both* (empathic response). *Let's sit down and talk about it* (broken record).

Peter: (Still pacing but more slowly now). *Talking is no good, I need help and I need it now.*

You: *I know you are in absolute despair because you are so tired and feel no-one is listening* (empathic response). *Come and sit down and we'll talk about it and find a way forward between us* (broken record).

Peter: (Calmer, finally sits down and for the first time gives you eye contact). *I can't go on like this.*

You: *I know you can't.*

In this scenario, calmly repeating the phrase *let's sit down and talk about it* is finally heard and responded to by Peter. Now he is able to listen and engage with you in finding a way forward, something that cannot be achieved while he is pacing the floor.

Fogging

Fogging can be a useful tool when the service-user is becoming aggressive and you are conscious of not inflaming the situation further. Fogging involves agreeing you can see the person's point of view without necessarily agreeing they are correct (McBride, 1998). Examples of fogging include the following:

- *That is a good point.*

- *I can see that you think I am…*

- *I can see you are angry about…*

A person who is being aggressive often invites an argumentative response in return and, of course, being argumentative usually inflames the situation. Agreeing you can see the protagonist's point of view can immediately defuse their aggression. Once the person is calmer, a more meaningful dialogue can then take place.

Service-user: *I've had nothing but bad service from you. You're never in when I phone you for help.*

Social worker: *I can see that you think I have let you down.*

Service-user: *I suppose you must be busy but I need some help.*

Social worker: *Let's work out what would help you most at the moment.*

It would be easy for the social worker in the above scenario to become defensive with the service-user. However, saying *I can see that you think I have let you down* acknowledges the person's distress without agreeing they are correct in this belief.

ACTIVITY *8.4*

Practise the techniques of using broken record *and* fogging.

- *Ask a friend to hold up and read a newspaper in a way that obscures their face from you. Try using the broken record technique, asking the person to put their newspaper down and listen to you. Repeat until the person responds.*

- *Now ask the person to either criticise or insult you in some way. Try responding using fogging.*

- *Ask your friend for feedback on your use of both techniques.*

COMMENT

Practising assertiveness techniques in role-play situations is a safe way of developing your skills. Remember we also explored using the Three-line Strategy *in Chapter 5. Just to remind you, this technique involves you first letting the service-user know you appreciate their position. Second, you state how you think or feel and, finally, you state what you would like to happen. With your newspaper reading friend, your response might be as follows:*

> I realise you really want some peace and quiet to read your paper, and I feel as if I am intruding on your space, but I would really like you to put the paper down and listen to me.

In the final section of this chapter, we will explore how the ending of the social work relationship can bring about feelings of anxiety and conflict for the service-user.

Ending the social work relationship

When service-users are desperate and over-reliant on the practitioner, conflict can arise when the social work relationship comes to an end. It is important to recognise that the service-user may have no one else in their lives to whom they can turn and these factors may make it difficult for the worker to resist requests for more and deeper involvement. Practitioners need to recognise the dangers of being drawn in too deeply and to be able to end relationships professionally and sensitively.

RESEARCH SUMMARY

Being self-aware, establishing and keeping boundaries and helping service-users to stay in control are all important factors when managing endings. The following pointers are taken from an article by Lombard et al. (2010) and can assist in planning endings with service-users.

Use self-awareness
- *Understand how personal experiences of endings may affect how we work, for example, a difficult ending in my own life may lead me to rescue service-users rather than assist them to help themselves.*

- *Recognise the power of transference (how the service-user may experience us similarly to other authority figures in their lives, for example, by expecting us to tell them what to do) and counter-transference (how they may remind us of someone in our own life and we unconsciously respond to this).*

- *Be willing to explore in supervision how our character traits may affect our boundaries. For example, do we need to be needed and will we consequently find it difficult to let go?*

Continued

RESEARCH SUMMARY continued

State boundaries

- *At the beginning of the work, clearly state what your role and boundaries are. Recognise the difference between adopting a friendly approach and being a friend.*

- *Establish clear objectives and planned outcomes including an ending. Concentrating on these helps to maintain focus and reduces the temptation to just chat.*

- *Throughout the work, remind service-users regularly of boundaries and, later, that the ending is approaching.*

- *Be mindful of any agency policy on time-limited working and work towards the ending by planning it together if possible. The more service-users feel in control of the ending the less likely they are to experience it as a rejection.*

Help service-users to stay in control

- *Establish from the beginning that this is not an open-ended relationship and that the aim of your work together is to help the service-user to take more control of their own life.*

- *Review progress regularly.*

- *Recognise, encourage and praise the service-user's progress and developing strengths.*

- *Acknowledge that the service-user is likely to find endings difficult: you have built up a working relationship with them and they will worry about losing your support. Also, you may worry about them.*

- *Plan with the service-user how they will access support once your relationship is ended.*

It is important when ending relationships with service-users to use empathic skills to try and understand their feelings about the event. Gentle challenging skills, assertiveness and helping the person to make future plans are all important too.

CHAPTER SUMMARY

In this chapter, we have seen that conflict is frequently experienced in social work practice. Sometimes, working with conflict leaves us vulnerable to physical attack and, of course, in these circumstances we must take appropriate action to protect ourselves. However, there are other instances when we can engage productively with people who are angry and, with a sensitive use of skills, we can often assist people to become calmer. Often, service-users' first contact with social workers is when they are scared, vulnerable and not in control of their own lives. While aggression can never be excused, we can engage with some of the reasons why people become aggressive. By recognising that fear, loss and not being heard can all precipitate anger we can help people to feel listened to when they express these emotions. Using empathy to place ourselves in the shoes of the other person can help us to better understand their anger. Combining empathy with self-awareness, skills from Transactional Analysis and assertiveness techniques can help us to recognise the early stages of aggression and defuse potentially dangerous situations. We need to try to understand and work alongside a service-user who is angry and recognise that this will be more productive than trying to control or ignore the anger.

Faulkner, A (1998) *When the news is bad: A guide for health professionals*. Cheltenham: Stanley Thornes.

Chapter 2, Breaking bad news, and Chapter 3, Picking up the pieces, are especially useful chapters in this informative and helpful book.

McBride, P (1998) *The assertive social worker*. Aldershot: Arena.

This whole book is recommended because it describes some excellent assertiveness techniques and also includes many helpful self-development exercises.

Rew, M and Ferns, T (2005) A balanced approach to dealing with violence and aggression at work. *British Journal of Nursing*, 14 (4): 227–32.

This article focuses on working with aggressive and angry patients and offers a very good overview of research in this field which is absolutely relevant to social work situations.

Taylor, BJ (2011) *Working with aggression and resistance in social work*. Exeter: Learning Matters.

The whole of Taylor's book is very informative and blends the practice and theory of working with angry service-users. Chapter 2, Understanding aggression and resistance, and Chapter 3, Avoiding assault and defusing aggression, are particularly relevant.

Chapter 9
Counselling skills in groupwork

Introduction

In this chapter, we will explore how to apply the interpersonal skills practised in earlier chapters to working with groups. Working with individuals requires us to focus on two things: what is happening to one other person and also our own process of thinking, feeling and behaviour. Facilitating groups requires us to focus on the thinking, feelings and behaviour of a number of individuals at the same time. Some group members may be colluding with each other, i.e. agreeing with each other to attain approval, and others may be competing with each other. Effective groupwork skills consist of listening and demonstrating we are listening to each member, empathic responses which are devoid of collusion, and techniques of encouraging individual group members to hear and acknowledge each other. An understanding of the stages through which groups can progress is also helpful and in this chapter we explore Tuckman's (1965) theory of group stages. We will also identify particular skills that can help groups to move through the various stages. Families, of course, are groups and the final section of this chapter will explore working in this setting. The Professional Capability Framework includes group facilitation and this chapter will help you to meet this competence.

What is a group?

Groups take many forms and most people belong to many groups. Some small groups you will work with will already be formed, such as family groups. Others will be newly formed groups, such as a parenting skills group. Thomas (1967, cited in Brown, 1994, p5) defines a small group as consisting of between three and twelve people and as *a collection of individuals who are interdependent with one another and who share some conception of being a unit distinguishable from other collections of individuals.* In social work you are likely to facilitate small groups (including talking to an individual with their family present) and in this chapter we will explore skills that can help you in this process.

Examples of groups with which you might be involved include:

- families;
- working groups with colleagues;
- student groups – for seminars, presentations, research;
- social groups – friends, activities, hobbies;
- supervision groups;
- residents' groups;
- support groups such as those which help with particular illnesses, difficult situations (such as domestic violence) and psychological problems, etc.

ACTIVITY 9.1

- *List all the groups with which you may be involved in relation to social work (including those associated with your course and placement).*
- *Identify your roles in each group.*
- *What responsibilities do you have within each role?*

COMMENT

It is likely that you are involved with many different types of groups associated with social work. You may have more than one role and these are likely to range from being a team member through to being a facilitator and you may believe that different roles attract a different level of responsibility. However, in a group which is performing at a high level, the boundaries between facilitator and group member are not so clear cut. In the next section, we will investigate how and why this may be the case by exploring Tuckman's work on the stages through which many groups progress.

RESEARCH SUMMARY

Tuckman's (1965) development sequence in small groups

Although Tuckman wrote his definitive study so long ago, it is still relevant and useful today (Lindsay and Orton, 2011; Preston-Shoot, 2007). Tuckman devised his theory from 50 articles on stages of group development. His findings were that groups have four clear stages, which he named forming, storming, norming *and* performing. *Later, Tuckman and Jensen (1977) added a fifth stage,* mourning, *which is characterised by the feelings of loss participants feel when groups are disbanded.*

Forming: Orientation, testing and dependence

Forming *takes place in the early stages of the group when people are finding their feet and getting to know other group members. Most people are polite and nervous with each other and there is a process of weighing up who is in the group. There is dependency on the facilitator, with group members seeking a response to issues from the leader. It is a phase of high anxiety, especially where group members feel their competency is on show (Lindsay and Orton, 2011; Preston-Shoot, 2007). Some thoughts which go through participants' minds in this stage include the following:*

- *What kind of group will it be?*
- *Who will have authority?*
- *How will people behave?*
- *Who is in charge?*
- *What will the leader be like?*
- *How much/little am I to be managed?*
- *What is my status in relation to the others?*
- *How much of myself will I have to give?*
- *How well will I be taken care of?*
- *Will there be any fun/humour in the group?*
- *Who might I like/dislike/fight/avoid/make friends with?*

Storming: Intragroup conflict and emotional responses to task demands

Once group members have got to know each other a little, the group often moves into this difficult stage (Lindsay and Orton, 2011). The storming *stage is characterised by dependence, resistance and hostility, rivalry for power and conflict between group members who compete with each other and polarise themselves into separate camps. In this stage, members may express concern about leadership, membership and authority and criticise and verbally attack the leader. Some individuals may dominate discussions unchallenged while others sit back and complain behind their backs. Individual members may be ridiculed in public and the rest of the group expects the facilitator to take control when this happens. The* storming *stage is unpleasant because it consists of distrust and bad feeling. In many instances, the group does not progress beyond this stage.*

Continued

RESEARCH SUMMARY *continued*

Norming: Development of group cohesion and open exchange

In this stage, there usually follows a process of reconciliation. Members have found their position in the group and start to feel that they belong. There is the beginning of a sharing of leadership between the facilitator and the group. The group tasks and the process (how the group is going to work together) largely can be discussed and agreed. There is a growing awareness of how one person's behaviour affects others and how this affects feelings. There is more support and cohesion and members take more responsibility with a willingness to examine what is happening in the group. Any new conflict is often suppressed at this stage because group members want to feel united and do not wish to revisit a previous painful stage. This suppression of anger may cause further problems.

Performing: Functional role-relatedness and emergence of solutions

Tuckman (1965) described the norming *stage as where cohesion is developed, whereas he saw the* performing *stage as consisting of the use of cohesion. Performing is the most productive stage and characterised by insight into the interpersonal process. The group realises its power and potential and recognises and accepts each member's strengths and weaknesses. Differences of opinion are no longer seen as 'rocking the boat' but are listened to and appreciated. The strength of the group exists, plus individuals are seen as individuals and accepted as such. Conflict is not feared but is worked through by listening and finding a compromise. More risks are taken by group members because a trust is in place which means there is no fear of being ridiculed or patronised. The group can now address the task because interpersonal issues have been resolved.*

ACTIVITY **9.2**

Think of a group of which you are a member.

- *Which of Tuckman's stages do you think applies to the group?*
- *Describe how group members are behaving.*
- *Now describe your own behaviour in the group.*
- *How does your behaviour help or hinder the group's development?*

COMMENT

My experience of working with groups is that the storming *stage is the most common, with few groups reaching the* performing *stage. A common response in the* storming *stage is to blame others for the state of the group. Where individuals are willing to look at their own motives and behaviour, this can propel the group into* norming. *Hough (2001) writes that each stage of development leaves groups faced with different problems and in the next section we will explore skills for helping groups move through the various stages.*

Skills for helping a group to *form*

Group members are often nervous in newly formed groups and it is the role of the facilitator to help people to get to know each other and feel as safe as possible in the group. If group members already know each other, a clear purpose and boundaries for the new group need to be established which separate the group from other walks of life (Brown, 1994).

Facilitate needs and expectations

Ice-breaking exercises during the first session can be helpful in the *forming* stage. Asking the group to write down their hopes and fears can be helpful because it quickly becomes apparent that others have the same or similar concerns. The next step is to produce a list of ground rules from the hopes and fears. Expectations of the purpose of the group need to be made clear by the members (Brown, 1994).

Offer warmth and appropriate self-disclosure

Group members will be weighing up the facilitator from the beginning, so it is important that you are aware of how you portray yourself. We explored warmth in Chapter 2 and commented on how warmth needs to be sincere: in other words, the facilitator must want to be there and be interested in the new group. Offering intimacy does not mean baring your soul. It means using appropriate self-disclosure to help the group to feel more comfortable with each other (Hough, 2001). For example, with a *forming* group, the facilitator might say:

- *I often feel quite nervous during the first session of a new group.*

- *When I think about ground rules, what is important to me is feeling that what is said in this room stays in this room.*

If the facilitator relates their own feelings to the group (as well as thoughts), the group then often feels permission to express their feelings too.

Demonstrate concern for others

During interactions it is important to demonstrate concern for, and include, all group members. Lindsay and Orton (2011) emphasise the importance of 'tuning in' to what we are feeling and also of communicating compassion to group members. It is easy for people to feel left out and sidelined and part of our role as facilitator is to notice and act when this happens. Maintaining eye contact helps the person to feel listened to and keeping the focus on one person at a time is essential if everyone is to feel included.

Listen and value each contribution

Active listening skills are essential when facilitating groups. Remember, in earlier chapters we defined active listening as listening *and demonstrating you are listening* to people. In group work, we need to paraphrase and use empathic responses with individuals equally in the group to demonstrate understanding of what they are saying and also to convey this understanding to the rest of the group. It is important in the *forming* stage to enable people to disclose their anxieties because they need to feel safe to participate in the group. In many groups, individuals unfortunately will be used to not feeling heard and therefore group members also need to be encouraged to listen to each other.

CASE STUDY

Listening to and valuing contributions

Imagine you are leading a support group for carers whose partners have dementia. Members are talking about their different experiences.

Ellen: My husband James has just been diagnosed and I'm really scared about what is going to happen to him. He is struggling to make himself understood and I have to do all the driving now because he just isn't safe on the road any more.

As soon as Ellen pauses, Cath then starts talking about her own husband:

Cath: My husband Frank is far worse than that. I have to wash and dress him and I can't remember the last time we had a proper conversation.

As the facilitator, you will want both group members to be able to have their say – but also to be able to engage with each other. You need to listen to and value each contribution and encourage both people to feel heard:

You: Cath, you are having a very tough time with Frank and I know you feel the responsibility is all on your shoulders. I'd like us to return to Ellen and then we'll come back to you. Ellen, it must be so hard for you to see James losing the ability to do things he has done all your married life…

Skills for helping a group move through the *storming* stage

Some groups stay in the *forming* stage throughout the whole time they are together. However, most groups move into the *storming* stage sooner or later and many groups do not move on from this stage, making it an uncomfortable experience for all members, including the facilitator. The more highly structured the group, the slower will be the movement through *storming* because, where there is any dissent, *storming* group members will turn to you as the facilitator to rescue them. You might choose to engage a co-facilitator during this stage because this process may be very challenging for one facilitator to manage. If we regard conflict as inevitable in groups (Hough, 2001), then perhaps we will anticipate it happening and manage it more effectively.

To help a group move through the *storming* stage, the facilitator can use the following skills.

Uncover, listen to and explore concerns

If difficulties are suppressed, deep fissures can appear making it difficult for the group to make any progression. Preston-Shoot (2007) states that the group leader needs to avoid giving solutions and instead provide a space where issues can be explored. One way concerns can be uncovered and listened to is via a group exercise called *Fear in a Hat* (Brandes, 1979). Each group member is given a blank piece of paper and a pen. They write down a fear or worry they have about working in the group (anonymously). Each piece of paper is folded up, placed in a hat and mixed around. One person at a time takes out a paper, unfolds and reads it out aloud. The matter on the paper is discussed. Often, similar themes emerge and the group learns that a number of people share the same concern. The group can become stronger after a calm and open discussion of the various topics.

Acknowledge the storming

Even if you do not use an exercise such as the one described above, at the very least you need to acknowledge that *storming* is happening in the group. Make sure you make observations rather than judgements:

What I noticed last week was that the group did not look comfortable with each other. Some people were sitting with their arms and legs crossed and were not giving anyone eye contact. I saw others huddled together but not engaging with the group. It feels as if there are lots of feelings stirring just below the surface. What do you think?

Of course, you may uncover some difficult feelings and dynamics within the group and you will need to be ready for the consequences. A *storming* group may turn on you (Tuckman, 1965) and it is important not to reply to this with a defensive response. Instead, continue with your observations of what is happening:

That's interesting. I am seeing individuals in the room who are clearly angry with one another but perhaps do not feel able to share those feelings with each other. Instead, the anger seems to be directed at me as the facilitator. Some of you are saying that I should have a word privately with certain individuals to make them behave. I think it would be useful for us to explore what we think are our responsibilities in the group and why we feel angry.

Self-disclosure of feelings

Here, the facilitator may use congruence – revealing their internal and external experiences – to disclose the effect the *storming* is having on them, for example:

Last week I found it really difficult to get any of my points across because other people continually spoke over me. In the end I felt like clamming up, did anyone else feel the same?

Owning up to a difficult feeling may offer permission for others to assert something similar.

Use listening skills to help group members to hear each other

As the facilitator, you will of course be using your listening skills. When the group is *storming,* however, you need to help members to listen to and acknowledge each other's viewpoints:

Group member X: *Nobody likes me in this group.*

Group member Y: *That's not true. We like to have a bit of fun with you but you can't take it.*

Facilitator: *X is saying she feels lonely and isolated in this group but you seem to be saying this is her fault.*

Y: *That feels harsh. I didn't mean to blame X. I don't think I realised before how she feels. I'm sorry X.*

Assertiveness and conflict management skills

Managing conflict in groups requires similar skills to those you would use with individuals. You need to utilise the challenging skills you learned in Chapter 5. Remember, good challenging skills involve empathic responding, active listening and assertiveness skills.

Imagine that for a few weeks now we have been facilitating the carers' group whose members' partners have dementia. There are eight people in the group and Cath has taken an increasingly dominant role each week. She talks a great deal and is not giving other members a chance to speak. At one point, when Ellen starts talking, Cath interrupts and tells Ellen she ought to think herself lucky that her husband is only in the early stages of dementia. Ellen looks as if she might cry. Tackling dominant members of groups is never easy. Brown (1994) suggests there are different responses which can be considered, including speaking directly to the individual within the group and speaking to the whole group. Koprowska (2010) tells us we need to maintain a good balance between individual needs and group needs. Whittaker (1985) writes that if we address the individual in the group, then this will also have an impact on other members too and we need to be mindful, therefore, of how we challenge. The *Three-line Strategy,* which we explored in Chapter 5, can be helpful to use here. As a reminder, the three stages are: identify with the other person; say how you feel; and state what you want. We do not wish to alienate Cath but we need to help her to see the effect she is having on other group members including Ellen:

Speaking directly to the individual during the groupwork
Cath, it must be very lonely and hard for you now that Frank needs you to give him so much care and what seems to be upsetting you most in the group is that some other members are not yet having to cope with the level of dementia that you are experiencing with Frank (identify with the other person). *I feel anxious because the aim of the group is for everyone here to be able to share their feelings and experiences* (state how you feel or what you think). *You have such a lot of experience of dementia to draw on and I'm wondering if you can think of ways to help the group members who are not quite so far down the road as you are with Frank* (state what you want).

According to Brown (1994), a problem with addressing the individual within the group is that it may alienate them further. He suggests that, wherever possible, facilitators should address the whole group because by doing this you encourage all the group members to take responsibility for what happens in the group.

Speaking to the whole group by reflecting back observations

I wonder if it might be useful to have a little time out from our task and explore what might be happening in our group. What I am seeing is a few people who seem to be talking a great deal and other group members who feel sidelined when they do get a chance to speak. I'm aware that people might be becoming upset. I'd like us to find out what we all think is happening and try and find a way forward that is better for everyone in the group. Who would like to start us off?

Of course, if the dominant members of the group begin to take over the discussion, the facilitator would need to limit their contribution and make space for the quieter members to contribute. The *broken record* technique from Chapter 8 (where we repeat our message) can help us here too:

Thanks for your contribution Cath but I'm going to stop you there because Ellen has something to contribute too… I'm going to stop you now because it's Ellen's turn… It's Ellen's turn… I'd like us to listen to Ellen.

Give constructive feedback by confronting individuals with the consequences of their behaviour and guiding them to look for alternative ways of resolving difficulties

If the person who is being disruptive does not respond to being challenged within the group, then your only remaining alternative may be to talk to them individually outside the group and determine between you a suitable course of action. Again, try to use empathy and challenging skills to establish the best way forward:

Cath, you have so much on your plate in looking after Frank. I can see from the groupwork the stress that you are under and I wonder if this comes out sometimes as resentment towards people whose partners are not as disabled as Frank is. It is absolutely understandable that you have a great deal to say and I am thinking that the group is perhaps not the best environment for you at the moment because you need more than the group can provide. My feeling is that it might be better for you to talk to someone about your situation on a one-to-one basis. What do you think would help you most at the moment?

Leaving the decision making as much as possible with Cath can help her to remain more in control and specify what her needs are.

Skills for *norming* and *performing*

If group members have moved through the *storming* stage, this means they are each taking more responsibility for themselves and their actions. Once this happens, the group moves forward into *norming* and *performing*. The facilitator's role is to encourage group members to continue to engage with each other. In the *norming* stage, when group members wish to suppress new conflict, your role is to help people to express calmly what is going on for them, assisting them to bring their fears into the open for discussion and resolution. In the *performing* stage, the group members become co-facilitators in their own development and do not look to you for the guidance they did earlier in the proceedings. Your role now is to help the group to sustain their engagement and to move forward if slippage occurs. Tuckman (1965) states that groups do move backwards and forwards along the continuum of formation and, indeed, he comments that each time the group meets, the whole process may start again.

RESEARCH SUMMARY

Tuckman's sequential model of group development is not without its critics. Preston-Shoot (2007) argues that one phase that is often missed out of staged models is that of revision. This stage would involve revisiting topics such as group aims, structure, methods and the way the group functions. It would also include reviewing progress and assessing whether a change in method is required. Doel (2006) argues that groups do not progress in a sequential manner through a staged process and that development generally takes place in a more erratic manner. Sutherland and Stroots (2010) experience Tuckman's model as being more cyclical rather than sequential in that group members re-visit the storming stage at different times. However, they found that having named stages is helpful in understanding and analysing group dynamics.

ACTIVITY 9.3

How skilled do you think you would be in helping a group to move through the storming stage?

- *What particular skills have you developed?*
- *What skills do you need to work on?*
- *How will you work on skills needed?*

COMMENT

This is a good place to take stock of your skill development. The more specific you can be about the skills you need to develop, the more likely you are to develop some well-crafted strategies.

Working with family groups

Families take on many forms and the skills required for working with them are not to be underestimated. Complex and therapeutic family work is a specialist area and needs to be undertaken by skilled, experienced and post-qualified family workers and is not something which social workers in training or newly qualified staff should undertake. However, there is a difference between family therapy and family work and there are likely to be occasions when we might find ourselves working with small family groups; for example, working with a bereaved family or doing a family assessment. O'Sullivan (1994) suggests it is appropriate to work with families when one or more family members are experiencing a difficulty and when the family is willing to work on the problem. Working with family groups can enable members to discuss issues, focus on particular tasks and to work through change. Family groups are complex and are different from other groups because of their shared history, established patterns of relating and their emotional involvement with each other (O'Sullivan, 1994).

Terry is a social worker and educator who has much experience of working with families. I interviewed him to find out how using counselling skills may help practitioners to work with families.

EXTRACT FROM AN INTERVIEW WITH TERRY

Working with a family group is taxing in skill because the family exists with established dynamics and patterns which could have existed for generations. Family work is usually about relationships and communication problems. Families move through stages and encounter different challenges at different points in the family life cycle e.g. adjusting to the birth or death of members. Loss can be a common issue in families which reverberates through the whole family system. Relationships between parents and children can also change as children grow up and there can be problems coping with ageing parents.

There can be a lack of effective communication within families where members do not understand or listen to each other. You need to try to facilitate the family to communicate more effectively with each other by ensuring everyone has a turn to give their point of view and each member listens to what is being said.

It's about exploring and bringing out any underlying family dynamics or beliefs that can lie beneath family problems. For example, one child may feel another is the favourite – which may or may not be true. Once the family can see these dynamics they have a better chance of addressing them.

Family work also helps individual members to understand each other. The purpose of asking questions is not necessarily to provide information but to help the family talk and listen to each other.

Once you have established the family story, you can ask the whole family 'how would you want things to be?' The child might say 'I would like us to go out as a family more' and then you can help the family to identify strategies to achieve this.

There are caveats to working with families. The group may be large and you need to be skilled at handling aggression and containing anger. Emotions are often raw with feelings held in check under the surface which can suddenly explode. It is best to work with a co-worker. It is also important to remember professional codes of ethics which require you not to work above your competence level.

From Terry's comments we can recognise that the skills needed for family work consist largely of counselling skills. The importance of using these skills is substantiated by Koprowska (2010) who writes about the need to build an alliance with family members, and Geldard and Geldard (2009) who comment on the importance of helping families to disclose their issues and talk about their needs. These are skills with which you are already familiar. Terry also talked about exploring the family's beliefs and this equates to *telling the story* from Egan's (2010) Skilled Helper model stage one. Moving on to establishing what the family needs or wants in order to help them is the next stage, ending with strategies for achieving these goals. Family work, as with other group work, involves listening to each family member and enabling members to hear and engage with each other. Whittaker (1985) adds that while watching, listening and seeking to understand are essential skills, it is also important to maintain a clear sense of the purpose of the group. This again matches Egan's idea of moving forward to action at all times.

Family work requires a high level of skill and when complex family work is needed specialist training will be involved. However, there will be occasions when non-specialists will be able to use their skills; for example, when working with parents and children to help them to engage with each other. Facilitating all types of groups is always a difficult and challenging task. Whittaker (1985) suggests that if you are conducting this work on your own, it will be helpful to find a colleague or supervisor who can act as a consultant and sounding board for you. Co-facilitating groups with a colleague where you can de-brief each session afterwards (talk about what went well and what could have been improved) is a good way to help you develop your skills for future sessions.

CHAPTER SUMMARY

Successful facilitation of both established and new groups is complex and demanding and requires high levels of interpersonal skill from practitioners. My experience of managing groups is that only a minority actually make it to the *performing* stage because the level of interpersonal skills required from each member is so high. In the *performing* stage, members are required to accept fully each other's strengths, weaknesses, quirks and foibles. Group members need to be able to hear and acknowledge others' strong feelings and to be skilled in expressing their own points of view assertively and non-judgementally. As we have seen from previous chapters, developing such skills to a high degree is a complex process.

Many groups that we work with will be encountered in the *storming* stage and much of our time as facilitator will be spent helping the group to move forward into a better, calmer and more productive stage. Again, skills explored in previous chapters such as empathic listening skills, challenging and assertiveness techniques can help us to successfully manage groups.

Working with conflicted families is a skilled and specialised area which usually requires post-qualifying training. If this chapter has whetted your appetite for furthering your knowledge of this area, a good place to start is to seek out opportunities to observe in practice colleagues who are qualified and skilled in this field.

In group work (as in all aspects of social work) it is important not to work above your competence level. One way you can develop your skills in facilitating groups is to co-facilitate with an experienced group worker whenever you can. Learning first-hand from someone who is able to respond effectively to the many challenges inherent in groupwork can be highly beneficial.

Hough, M (2001) *Groupwork skills and theory*. London: Hodder and Stoughton.

This is a very readable book which is packed full of information about useful skills for groupwork. Chapter 4, How groups develop, and Chapter 5, The leader and the group, are particularly useful.

Houston, G (1990) *The red book of groups*. 3rd edition. Norfolk: The Rochester Foundation.

This little book has become a time-honoured classic. It is short and down-to-earth and the author shares her considerable experience of group facilitation.

Koprowska, J (2010) *Communication and interpersonal skills in social work*. 3rd edition. Exeter: Learning Matters.

Chapter 7, Working with families and groups, is highly informative. It defines different kinds of families, explores how to work with family groups and describes recent initiatives such as *family group conferencing*.

Lindsay, T and Orton, S (2011) *Groupwork practice in social work*. 2nd edition. Exeter: Learning Matters.

This book focuses on groupwork in social work and is a practical hands-on guide to working in this area. Chapter 3, Facilitation and co-facilitation, and Chapter 5, Group processes, are particularly recommended.

Preston-Shoot, M (2007) *Effective groupwork*. 2nd edition. Basingstoke: Palgrave Macmillan.

This is a comprehensively written and informative book. Chapter 7, Working with groups, focuses on useful skills for group facilitators.

Relate. www.relate.org.uk

Relate has an excellent website that contains much information relevant to working with couples and families. The section on *common problems* offers some excellent guidance on a number of areas such as coping with a new baby and coping with disruptive teenagers.

Tuckman, B (1965) Developmental sequence in small groups. *Psychological Bulletin*, 63 (6): 384–99.

Tuckman's original work is still available and is readable and informative. His theory stands the test of time and is as helpful now as it was in the 1960s.

Chapter 10
Counselling skills in different settings

Introduction

This chapter will begin by summarising the toolkit of counselling skills which you have already developed. We will then explore the kinds of difference which may exist in the lives of service-users. There will then be an exploration of additional skills which can help us to communicate with people when working in a variety of specialist settings: working with children and young people; working with people with disabilities; learning difficulties; and working with older people. Each person with whom we work is a unique individual. We must be careful not to treat service-users in a stereotypical manner. A common pitfall is to make assumptions about service-users because we have classified the person as belonging to a particular group. For example, if we know a new service-user who we are about to meet is 90 years old, would we speak with a raised voice in the expectation that she is bound to be deaf? We need to learn from the service-user in front of us about their *own* culture, life and experience and see them as the unique individual that they are. However, we also need to be mindful of various factors which can help us too and this chapter will explore some of these areas.

Toolkit of skills and using the Egan model creatively

The skills which you have been encouraged to develop throughout this book are all necessary to working in the areas listed above. The Egan (2010) model, as we have seen in previous chapters, offers a framework for using counselling skills in multiple settings. Remember, whatever the setting we need to help each person to express what is going on for them now (stage one), tell us what they need or want (stage two) and work out how they are going to get there (stage three). In previous chapters, we have focused on verbal methods of establishing these three stages. However, we can also use non-verbal methods to help service-users. For example, we could ask a child to draw or paint three pictures. In the first, the child could depict what is going on for them now, the second could be a picture of how they would like their life to be and the final drawing or painting could consist of all the things that would help them to achieve what they want or need.

It is useful to remember that Rogers' (1961) core conditions are relevant to working with all service-users. In each case we need to express warmth, empathy, unconditional positive regard and congruence and we may need to work hard to demonstrate these skills clearly. For example, an older person with memory loss might be feeling a heightened state of anxiety because of their difficulties in finding the words to express to us their wishes and feelings. In this instance, it is very important not to rush them and to provide plenty of time and space and to pace the session to match the needs of the service-user.

We need to help each person to tell their own, unique story (not necessarily verbally, as we will see later). Where the service-user can't find the right words or is unable to use verbal forms of communication because they have, for example, dementia or aphasia, then we need to focus on and interpret accurately the message being conveyed to us by the service-user.

We also need to be able to identify the person's own wishes. Becoming skilled in identifying and tuning into each person's form of communication and interpreting what they are trying to convey to us may require us to undertake specialist training and to work closely with practitioners who are already skilled in their particular field. At the very least, we need to guard against believing that ascertaining the wishes and feelings of someone who communicates non-verbally, or who has difficulty with verbal communication, is a simple task. Neither can we be complacent in thinking that following one model of engaging will prepare us for every eventuality. Remember, *every* person with whom we work is an individual with a unique history and specific and individual needs. We need to use all the skills we possess, and sometimes engage in additional training to develop these further, to find out what is happening to the service-user now, what they want or need and how they are going to be helped to achieve this.

Exploring difference in the lives of service-users

There is a contradiction in this chapter because I have begun by writing about the importance of seeing the service-user as a unique person and I have then raised the topic of working with people who belong to different groups (such as older people, etc.). Fook (2002, p51) describes this as the *dilemma of difference,* which means that if we identify and place people into particular categories of groups, how do we make sure we do not stereotype or stigmatise them?

Barna (1994, p337) examines this same argument in his exploration of working with people from different cultures. He argues that we need to realise that we are *all culturally bound and culturally modified.* In other words, we all behave in ways which are consistent with our culture and, at the same time, we have our own individual ways of being too. We therefore need to recognise where cultural aspects exist and at the same time see where people's individual characteristics are different from this culture. This concept can be applied to working with people from other groups too, for example, older people. Recognising that service-users are both *group bound* and *group modified* can help us to see the whole person more clearly. If we begin by expecting the service-user to have individual differences from the group to which we perceive them belonging, then we are less likely to fall into the trap of making assumptions about them. To help us with this, Bethell and O'Sullivan (2010, p15) offer three *health warnings* for us to remember:

1. Respect people as unique human beings while appreciating those parts of a person's self-identity which are involved in group identification.

2. Take care not to apply crude labels or reinforce stereotypes when we use categories to analyse difference.

3. Do not lose sight of the complex multiple nature of identity when focusing on one category of difference.

An important point is to remain focused on our own reactions and responses to difference. Fook (2002, p83, citing Minow, 1985) suggests the following:

Locate the problem of difference squarely in the relationships which define the difference, rather than in the difference itself. The problem is in the way we construct difference, rather than being inherent to the differences we identify.

In working with difference then, it is important that we can identify our own stereotypical ways of thinking and understand how these become barriers to engagement. Developing this level of self-awareness is not easily achieved alone. Good supervision is critical here because it helps us to challenge our blind spots, to interpret astutely and to see the real service-user rather than see only our assumptions of the service-user. Now we have established this very important point, we can explore further some useful ways of working which may help us when engaging with service-users from different groups.

Working with children and young people

Children often feel overpowered by adults but may not wish to show this and such feelings are likely to be exacerbated when young people engage with social workers (Woodcock Ross, 2011; Lefevre, 2010; Koprowska, 2010). When a child feels overwhelmed they are less likely to be able to communicate fully what is happening for them. Children, like adults, need to be helped to feel safe before they will disclose information to a social worker. Woodcock Ross (2011) notes that feeling unsafe with adults was a key element which stopped Victoria Climbié from disclosing abuse to her social workers. Building an effective working relationship with a child is therefore very important in helping the young person to develop trust. Woodcock Ross (2011) also notes that knowledge of theories which underpin child development, such as attachment theory, is essential when building relationships with children. If a child feels insecure with their parent or caregiver, they are likely to transfer this feeling onto other significant adults such as their social worker. Woodcock Ross states that transference may manifest in the child wanting to please the social worker or in feeling overly anxious.

We need to use a range of counselling skills to help children to develop trust in us. However, we also need to be congruent with children because we may not use the information in a way they would like us to, for example, in seeking their removal from home if they are being abused. In the next section we will explore particular counselling skills which can help us to communicate more effectively with children.

Skills for working with children and young people

When children and young people seek help, professionals frequently respond in a manner which displays power and authority over the young person. Gordon (1974, cited in Oliver and Pitt, 2011) states that when young people convey unhappiness, professionals often respond by ordering, moralising, preaching, analysing or giving solutions. These approaches are all barriers which must be avoided. Instead, we need to use empathic responding. Placing ourselves in the shoes of the young person and trying to understand what they are experiencing can help them to feel understood and in control (Woodcock Ross, 2011). In addition to empathy, Koprowska (2010) suggests also using the following ways of working with young people:

• Use clear and simple communication.

• Follow the child's lead rather than direct them.

• Go at the child's pace.

• Be aware that you may be required to communicate with other people around the child.

- Use age-appropriate questions: by the age of three years children can usually understand what is meant by *what, who* and *where;* by three and a half they can usually understand *how to do* but not *how often;* by age five they usually understand *when;* and by age eight, they usually understand *why.*

- Be comfortable in using play to communicate.

We also need to be mindful when talking to children of respecting particular boundaries. For example, we may need permission from their parents or caregivers to talk with the child. We also need to specify to the child what we can and cannot keep confidential regarding any disclosure they may make.

Children may not have the vocabulary to describe to us how they are feeling or what is happening to them so we may need to use more creative methods to help them to tell their story and convey to us what they want or need. Using play may be a new area for us in which to develop skills. Play may provide ways for the child to uncover feelings of past, present and future (Koprowska, 2010; Watts and Garza, 2008; Quackenbush, 2008). Koprowska suggests we keep at our disposal a range of objects to help us in this process, such as soft toys, small figures, puppets, toy telephones, paper and crayons, toy cars and play dough. She describes how a child may be able to describe how teddy might be feeling about an event much more easily than talking directly about their own feelings.

CASE STUDY

In this example, Elsa (aged six) has experienced the death three months ago of her maternal grandmother to whom she was very close. Her parents are worried about Elsa because she never talks about her grandmother or seems to express an emotion about her loss. She has recently started wetting the bed and is refusing food at meal-times, saying she is not hungry. Elsa's favourite toy is Benny, her fluffy rabbit. She has previously told the helper that she tells Benny all her secrets.

SW: Elsa, how is Benny feeling today?

Elsa: Benny is very sad today.

SW: Benny's very sad?

Elsa: Yes, Benny is very sad but he isn't crying.

SW: He feels very sad and it sounds as if he wants to cry but he is trying very hard not to.

Elsa: That's right, he is being very brave. If he starts to cry, he will make mummy rabbit cry too and he doesn't want to make her feel sad as well.

In talking in the third person about her rabbit's feelings, Elsa demonstrates she feels that expressing emotion about her grandmother's death will make her responsible for upsetting her mum. She wishes to protect her mother from further hurt and does this by keeping her own emotions in check. Shutting down her emotions is taking a great deal of effort and her suppressed emotions manifest in wetting the bed and losing her appetite. Now Elsa's family understand what is happening for her, they can help her to express her emotions about her grandmother in a safe and accepting way.

Lefevre (2010) suggests using painting and drawing as a communication aid. She states that it is very important to proceed at the child's pace during this activity and to refrain from analysing what the child produces. In the case study above, Elsa could be asked to draw one picture of her life before Grandma died, and another picture of her life after Grandma has died. Mary, the hospice social worker who we met in Chapter 7, describes how she uses this technique to help children to express feelings about loss:

> *I once worked with a young boy whose painting of his life before his grandma died had a smiling sun, sand, blue sky and his family playing together. His second picture, depicting his family after grandma died, was very dark in colour, had rain, umbrellas and a frowning sun. The child was completely off to one side of the picture, isolated from the rest of his family. When the family saw the picture it gave them insight – they recognised how he was feeling and they all then worked together with him. A year later I asked the boy to paint another picture and this time the sun was again smiling and the family were together and again having fun. It was a very powerful experience for all of us. The family gave me the pictures and asked me to use them to help social workers in training.*

If Elsa, from the case study above, had drawn a similar picture, it would be important to enable her to tell us what was happening in it and for us to use empathic responses to help us both to understand its meaning. Lefevre suggests that we should comment neutrally on the shapes and colours used rather than question the child directly on the meaning of the picture. This helps the child to feel supported and connected to the picture:

SW: *Would you like to tell me what is happening in your pictures Elsa?*

Elsa: *In the first picture, we are all playing together on the beach and the sun is smiling. The second picture has bad things.*

SW: *In the first picture there are lots of bright colours and all the people look happy. In the second picture you have used lots of dark colours and I can see it raining down on people who have their umbrellas up.*

Elsa: *Yes. Everyone is very sad. They don't like the rain and they don't know when it is going to stop. The rain is making people nearly fall over.*

Leaving Elsa in control of what she talks about and using empathic responses helps Elsa to express her feelings in reference to her picture.

Lefevre (2010) proposes using an *ecomap*. This involves constructing a picture of how children perceive themselves in relation to the people around them. She suggests that the child either writes their name or draws a representation of themselves in the middle of a piece of paper. Then, significant others, represented as circles, are placed on the page around the young person. The child can then choose a method to demonstrate the closeness or otherwise of the relationship between themselves and the others on the page. They could choose, for example, different colours to denote different levels of closeness or different sorts of lines (for example, thick lines or dotted lines). Lefevre also suggests the child could instead use dolls, toy animals or different shaped buttons to make the relationship representations.

Genograms (McGoldrick et al., 2008) (see Chapter 7) can also be used in the same way. In practice, just writing someone's name can mean the service-user experiences feelings related to that person. The use of a genogram would mean that significant people who have left the family or died are also included.

ACTIVITY 10.1

- *How confident do you feel in using play and artwork to communicate with children?*

- *Construct your own ecomap or a genogram.*

- *What have you learned about yourself from this picture?*

- *What do you need to work on in your communication skills with children?*

COMMENT

Working with children involves skills which we have already developed and also some new skills such as creative play. If we do not have much contact with children in our own lives, then we might need to set some specific goals for our own development of skills in this area. Constructing our own ecomap or genogram can help us to see how powerful such exercises can be.

Using different art forms is a good way of encouraging children to communicate with us. Another method would be to use a set of soft toys to form a set of tableaux (a tableau being a still picture or representation). The child could arrange the toys to depict their life now, and again to demonstrate what they would like their life to be like. The final tableaux could consist of the soft toys demonstrating the strategies that would need to be in place to help the child to achieve their goals.

ACTIVITY 10.2

Paint or draw three pictures or use soft toys to form tableaux which represent your life now, how you would like it to be and, finally, what would help you to achieve your goal.

COMMENT

It does not matter if we are not very good at painting or drawing because what is most important is what the figures and shapes in the painting represent to us. Sometimes we can express more accurately what is going on for us in a form which is different from words.

Finding different and creative ways to communicate can also be very important when we work with people who have disabilities. In the next section we will explore further some of these ways of working.

Working with people who have physical disabilities

Working with people who have disabilities and their carers requires us not to lose sight of the approach we would use with people who do not have disabilities. We need to work with each person as an individual and not make assumptions about them because of their disability, although we do need to take their condition into account in our approach. We also need to be aware that people who we regard as having a disability may well not identify themselves in this category.

RESEARCH SUMMARY

Woodcock Ross and Tregaskis (2008) in their research on communication barriers experienced by the parents of disabled children found that what is important is for the social worker to listen to and find out the individual needs of each service-user. Practitioners should be mindful of the barriers they place in the way of effective communication and should strive at all times to bring these into conscious awareness and work so these cease to become barriers. Woodcock Ross and Tregaskis found that parents most value an active partnership with their social worker where both parties work with each other's expertise. The researchers recommend the following ways of working:

- *Discuss frankly the individual communication needs of the child.*

- *Recognise the private knowledge the person or their carer has of the child's particular difficulties.*

- *Be open to hearing new knowledge of the particular characteristics of the disability which relate to the person and reflect on our own ability to be open to this.*

- *Listen to and reflect back to the service-user and carers their difficulties, pain and frustration. This helps the person to talk freely without fear of judgement or blame. It also helps them to better understand what they are experiencing.*

The suggestions from Woodcock Ross and Tregaskis match the skills and ways of engaging with which you are already familiar. Although the research was undertaken with the families of children with disabilities, the principles can also be applied to wider situations. One such principle is the importance of the practitioner seeing service-users with disabilities in the same way as any other service-user: that is, as the expert on themselves. Another is being careful not to allow the disability to be a barrier to our communication skills. The practitioner needs to use empathic responding and active listening skills to learn from the person about their difficulties, frustrations, strengths and coping strategies. We need to recognise when we are stereotyping the service-user, e.g. when we make assumptions about what they can or cannot do. We do this when we see the person within the context of a group or category rather than as an individual. This failing is explored in the following case study.

CASE STUDY

Justine (a social worker in training) visits Diana, who is 70 years old. Diana is preparing for a week's stay in hospital where she is having a knee replacement. When Justine enquires about what support Diana has, she asks her if she has any children. Diana tells Justine she lives with her daughter, Anita, aged 45 who has been blind since birth. Diana invites Anita into the room to meet Justine. Justine assumes that Diana cares for Anita and is worried about who will look after Anita when Diana goes into hospital. She says to Anita, we will need to think about who is going to look after you when your mum goes into hospital. Anita replies that in fact Diana lives with her rather than the other way round and that her most pressing worry is arranging care for her mum when she is at work (Anita works full-time as a computer programmer). Justine soon realises she has stereotyped Anita in a number of ways. She has assumed that because Anita is blind and lives in the same house as her mum, Anita is completely dependent on her mum for care. It has not occurred to Justine that Anita will be taking on a caring role or that she has to balance these responsibilities with a full-time job.

It can be seen from the case study above that a major barrier to engaging with people with disabilities occurs when assumptions are made about what the person can and cannot do. Woodcock Ross (2011, p138) suggests the following ways of working with people with disabilities: *actively look for the channels of communication that the person is using and use the whole communication spectrum.* Woodcock Ross states that if we are to do this well we will need to plan a strategy beforehand of how we will communicate with the service-user. She states that this plan needs to include how we will work with a carer who feels the need to speak *for* the service-user instead of letting the service-user communicate their own wishes and feelings. Sometimes, however, the carer is the expert on the service-user, especially in methods of communication, and so we also need to recognise the occasions when the service-user would prefer us to talk to the carer.

ACTIVITY 10.3

Think of a time when you expected an individual to think, feel or behave in a particular way.

- *From where did your expectations arise?*
- *How did your assumptions affect your interaction?*
- *What did you learn?*

COMMENT

Challenging ourselves on the assumptions we make about individuals because we perceive them as belonging to a particular group is something we need to monitor. Maintaining an acute awareness of ourselves and our unconscious processes in this matter is vital if we are to challenge the assumptions we make.

In the next section, we will explore the use of communication and counselling skills with people who have learning difficulties.

Working with people who have learning difficulties

Many people who have learning difficulties are not used to exercising power and choice over their lives because they have been subjected to control by others (Williams, 2009). The term 'learning difficulties' encompasses a wide spectrum and, as such, it is again important that as practitioners, we do not make any assumptions in relation to people who may be identified in this way. If we are to communicate effectively with service-users who have learning difficulties we need to think about how we are going to hear their stories and establish what they want and need. Mencap holds wide resources for helping practitioners and families to better meet the needs of people with learning difficulties.

RESEARCH SUMMARY

Goldbart and Caton (2010) produced a report for Mencap which assessed approaches and techniques for communicating with people with complex needs. Their findings are that people with profound learning difficulties most often communicate via facial expressions and bodily movements rather than verbally and that it is important for social care workers to get to know the individual ways in which each service-user communicates. The authors interviewed parents to find out what helps them most in communicating with their family members and they also reviewed current literature and research. Their findings are that the following tools are helpful:

- *Objects of reference – using particular objects that are relevant. For example, showing the service-user part of a seat-belt to find out if the person wishes to go out in the car.*

- *A picture exchange communication system (PECS) – where the service-user exchanges a picture symbol for something that they want. Goldbart and Caton suggest this is particularly useful for working with children with autism.*

- *A signing system such as MAKATON, which enables people with learning difficulties to communicate using symbols.*

- *High-tech systems such as augmentation and alternative communication (AAC). This includes voice output communication aids (VOCAs) – computer software that involves accessing pre-recorded spoken or printed statements which can be accessed by pressing a switch.*

- *Pictures of symbols to communicate.*

The authors also suggest first taking time to get to know the service-user and becoming familiar with the way they communicate including taking advice from their family and, second, being consistent in approach. They highlight the importance of seeing the service-user as an individual with their own ways of communicating and emphasise the usefulness of the following ways of working:

Continued

- *Use short and simple phrases.*

- *Approach the service-user with warmth, for example, by smiling and giving a positive greeting. This reduces the power imbalance.*

- *Have a positive and caring attitude, be empathic and have the ability to form relationships.*

- *Help the service-user to identify choices.*

Goldbart and Caton also suggest using communication passports. *These are individual documents, which describe the uniqueness of the service-user. Millar (2006) has devised an excellent template for producing a communication passport. She suggests the average length of the document should be approximately 20 pages long and needs to include the person's name and how they like to be addressed, their likes and dislikes, how the person communicates and particular areas with which they need help.*

Mencap's website highlights that 55 per cent of a person's communication is through body language, 38 per cent via tone of voice and 7 per cent by words. They offer a wealth of helpful material for communicating with people with learning difficulties including the following suggestions:

- *Find a place to communicate which has no distractions.*

- *Ask open questions.*

- *Paraphrase to check understanding.*

- *Observe the person's body language and facial expressions.*

- *Learn from your experience.*

- *Take your time.*

- *Use gestures and facial expressions to clarify feelings, for example, if you are asking someone if they are unhappy, make an unhappy face when you ask the question.*

- *Try drawing to communicate.*

- *Use objects, photos and pictures.*

- *Use all of your communication tools.*

- *Follow the lead of the service-user.*

- *Go at the service-user's pace.*

Working with older people

Defining when an adult becomes an older person is not an easy or simple process. Negative attitudes to older people are common and people from this group are often stereotyped. Stuart-Hamilton (2011) states that people who have deep-rooted negative attitudes towards older people rarely see any positive aspects of ageing. When we are forming relationships with older service-users we need to begin by bringing into conscious awareness the assumptions we hold about older people. The following extracts are examples of comments made to me by older people:

> **V (63)**: *I can't stand the use of the term 'granny'. Where I work we have a 'fun day' once a year which involves outdoor games, activities and tombolas, etc. This year, someone had a sign up at one of the stalls which said 'granny sitting'. Why on earth would I need to be 'granny' sat?*

> **R (87)**: *My granddaughter accompanied me when I went to the doctor's recently. The doctor kept addressing my granddaughter instead of me. She was really incensed that he did not talk directly to me but to be honest, I barely noticed it, things like that happen all the time.*

> **M (70)**: *I've joined a night-class to learn French. It's something I've always wanted to do and now I have the chance. The person who enrolled me asked me if I would be able to learn a language at my age. It's as if some people think once you reach a certain age you are incapable of learning anything new.*

As we can see from the comments above, older people are frequently subjected to deep-seated and widespread prejudices and this can leave them feeling disempowered, angry and frustrated. When working with older people we need first to look deep within ourselves and confront our own prejudicial attitudes. Do I believe that an older person is set in their ways or incapable of learning new skills or is bound to be hearing impaired or will have some degree of dementia or is frail, lonely and weak?

ACTIVITY **10.4**

- *When do you think old age begins?*
- *How do you view someone who is 20, 30 or 40 years older than yourself?*
- *How was your view different when you were younger?*
- *What experiences have influenced your views of older people?*

COMMENT

Analysing our own attitude to age, ageing and any stereotypes we hold about older people is very important if we are to overcome barriers in communicating. We need to be especially careful when we catch ourselves saying well, older people, they all...don't they? *This means we are seeing the group rather than the individual person.*

Help the Aged (now Age UK) (2007) offers some very helpful points to remember when engaging with older people including the following dos and don'ts:

- Remember that older people are people.
- Use common courtesy and ask how the person wishes to be addressed.

- Avoid stereotyping: remember, 'older people' are just an older version of you (or the same age as you inside, they just look older).

- Respect the views of older people – mutual respect requires truthful dialogue.

- Always speak directly to the older person and not the person they are with (such as a carer or companion).

- Never assume that older people lack knowledge, or are incapable of assimilating information; they may (at times) be slower to assimilate, but that does not mean they cannot. On the other hand, don't assume too much knowledge: try to strike a balance.

Working with older people who have dementia requires us to be particularly *visibly tuned in* (Egan, 2010, p132) to the messages being conveyed and we will explore this area next.

Working with older people who have dementia

When we are engaging with older people who have dementia we need to be open to receiving communication in all its forms from the person. Woodcock Ross (2011, p169) suggests that we:

> *...seek out the channels of communication the person is using – to look for the feeling that is being articulated, even though the words may not be making any sense.*

Some channels of communication are more likely to be non-verbal and we need to observe these signs as closely as possible. Egan (2010) tells us that even when the service-user is silent, they will still convey to us strong messages via their facial expressions, bodily movement, tone of voice and responses to us. Egan notes that it is important to tune in to the following messages:

- Behaviour, such as posture, gestures and bodily movement.

- Eye behaviour, such as staring or removal of eye contact.

- Facial expressions: smiling, frowning, expression of fear, frustration, relief, etc.

- Tone of voice, such as volume, pitch, intensity, silence, spacing of words and what is emphasised.

- Physiological responses, such as breathing patterns, pupil dilation and blushing.

- Reaction to personal space, i.e. how close or far away is the person.

Being open to receiving the non-verbal messages from service-users with dementia is especially important because this may be their only way of communicating with us.

Tuning in to the service-user is only one half of the engagement process. Egan (2010) tells us also to develop awareness of our own non-verbal behaviour because the service-user will read these cues and interpret accurately the signals we are transmitting. A service-user who has dementia will be similar to other service-users in their need to feel confident in and trustful of their helper before they will be able to open up about what is happening for them. Woodcock Ross (2011) informs us that having dementia does not mean the service-user does not have wishes and feelings and that we need to find out what these are. She states that we need to identify the feeling that the person is communicating to us and reflect our understanding of this back to the service-user. Woodcock Ross suggests one way we can do this is to mirror the service-user's bodily movements back to them. When achieved sensitively, mirroring will indicate that we are trying to understand what is going on for the person.

Another area to be mindful of is that service-users with dementia may also suffer from physical difficulties such as hearing and sight impairments. Kiessling et al. (2003) suggest that impaired hearing can be exacerbated by impaired vision. This is because the non-verbal cues sought from the practitioner's facial expressions and gestures are not apparent to the person. Facial expressions which would indicate we might be speaking with irony or humour may not be seen by the service-user and they consequently miss the essence of what we are communicating. The researchers also found that it can be exhausting for older people with hearing impairment and cognitive impairments to concentrate for long periods on the speaker and this is compounded in noisy environments or when other people are also speaking. A person who has difficulty hearing may therefore tune out and decide not to listen in order to conserve their limited energy. We need to be mindful of these points when engaging with older people who have such impairments. Interpreting cues from service-users is important and we need to recognise when the person might be getting tired or finding it difficult to concentrate (perhaps because they are hungry or need the toilet). Using counselling skills of paraphrasing, reflecting, frequent summarising and keeping our questions short and open can all help the service-user to maintain their focus.

CASE STUDY

Joe is 85 and lives alone in a ground floor flat in a sheltered accommodation complex. He has no close family. Joe's hearing and vision have deteriorated in recent months and he is beginning to become forgetful. This morning, in the snow, Joe went out for some milk and became lost. He was brought back to his flat two hours later by the police who also arranged for Joe's social worker, Chris, to visit that afternoon. Chris makes sure he sits away from the window so Joe will be able to see him more clearly. He sits at the same level as Joe and adopts a SOLER (Egan, 2010) position.

Chris: I've called to see if you are OK after what happened this morning.

Joe: After what happened this morning?

Chris: I think you went out for some milk and lost your way home. The police brought you back home Joe.

Joe (looking agitated): The police. Yes, a nice woman helped me. I couldn't find my way back.

Chris: It must have been really frightening for you Joe (empathic response).

Joe: I was frightened. I was cold and I thought I was going to die. You're not going to make me leave here are you?

Continued

CASE STUDY *continued*

Chris: I can see how upsetting it is for you to have become lost this morning but it sounds as if what would be even more awful for you would be to lose your independence and move into residential care *(empathic response to convey to Joe an understanding of his feelings)*.

Joe: I couldn't stand it, being with all the old dears. That's not me.

Chris: You don't want to lose everything you have here. I am worried about you though Joe – it might happen again. You said you were worried you weren't going to make it back at all and that must have been terrifying *(empathy and challenge)*.

Joe: I'll be OK *(staring at the floor and squeezing his hands together tightly, his jaw is clenched)*. I don't want to move.

Chris (noticing Joe's body language and facial expression): Joe, I can see you don't want to move. But I also get the feeling that you are really scared about what will happen to you if you get lost again *(empathic response and challenge)*. If you were managing going out a bit better, what sort of things could you be doing that you are not doing now? *(Stage 2 future possibility question.)*

Joe: I'd still be living here and going out but I would be able to find my way back too.

Chris: It sounds as if what would help are some strategies in place to help you next time you go out *(paraphrasing Joe's wants and needs)*. What would help you to find your way back next time? *(Brainstorming strategies.)*

Joe: I could go out with my neighbour, oh, what is his name? He goes out every day.

Chris: Howard from next door? That sounds like a good way forward. Shall we talk to Howard about you going out with him next time?

Joe is adamant he wants to remain living independently and it is important that while Joe has capacity to make this decision that it is respected by Chris. Joe sees himself as less powerful than his social worker and he worries that Chris will make decisions for him. By Chris noticing Joe's body language and facial expressions and reflecting his understanding of what Joe is conveying in his non-verbal behaviour he helps Joe to feel understood. Chris uses lots of empathic responding and challenges Joe gently to look more realistically at his situation. By encouraging Joe to say what he wants and needs and to think of strategies which would help him to do this, he keeps the power of decision making with the service-user.

Working with people from different cultures

In social work we will communicate and engage with people from all kinds of cultures and backgrounds. Bethell and O'Sullivan (2010) state that one of the challenges of social work is to work with individuals as unique service-users while at the same time being respectful of the person's collective identity. Practitioners need to be culturally sensitive in their communication.

RESEARCH SUMMARY

Barna (1994) describes six stumbling blocks in intercultural communication.

1. **Assumption of similarities**: *there are no universal rules when it comes to interpreting body language, facial expressions and feelings.*

2. **Language differences**: *we need to be careful not to use slang or complicated sentence construction, for example, double negatives.*

3. **Non-verbal misinterpretations**: *we need to interpret the unspoken codes conveyed by people from other cultures and learn these. For example, in Korean culture, individuals often do not smile at each other unless they know the person well and may interpret smiling coming from a stranger in Western culture as suspicious.*

4. **Preconceptions and stereotypes**: *recognising when and how we stereotype people is important. Barna (p338) states that stereotypes persist because they are firmly established as myths or truisms by one's own national culture and they sometimes rationalise prejudices. We tend to select information that feeds our assumptions.*

5. **Tendency to evaluate**: *we need to guard against interpreting communication wrongly, for example, by assuming a person is being humorous when they are not.*

6. **High anxiety**: *a little anxiety on our part can alert us to difference. However, too much tension makes us defensive and stressed and when this happens we might misinterpret the service-user.*

Barna (1994) also states that in a new culture, service-users (such as asylum seekers) can experience culture shock. This may leave them feeling stressed, exhausted and less likely to trust and engage with helpers. Woodcock Ross (2011) emphasises how asylum seekers and refugees may experience acute psychological distress. This is likely to be as a result of their experiences of abuse before they migrated and profound loss since they arrived. We need to recognise how such distress might impact on the service-user's ability to engage with us and we may need to spend considerable time in building a relationship where the person gradually feels able to trust us.

CHAPTER SUMMARY

In social work interactions we need to build fruitful relationships with service-users from all different backgrounds. Using counselling skills well means striving to recognise and uphold the uniqueness of each service-user. Rogers (1961) called this process prizing the client and, indeed, if we are to work effectively with people who are different from ourselves, we need to be able to see the service-user as the complete individual which they are. It can also sometimes deepen our understanding of the service-user if we develop awareness of some particular factors which *may* be pertinent to particular groups or categories of service-users, for example, using age-appropriate questions with children.

We need to remain very much aware of the *dilemma of difference* (Fook, 2002), which means that if we are going to place service-users into particular groups then we need to make sure we do not stereotype or stigmatise them. Good supervision is crucial in helping us to balance this dilemma and keep the needs of each service-user at the centre of decision making.

Age UK website: www.ageuk.org.uk

This website contains a great deal of information which can help us to work with older service-users, including help-sheets and pointers to further research.

Fook, J (2002) *Social Work: Critical theory and practice*. London: Sage.

Chapter 6, Identity and Difference, explores how individual identity develops in the context of social structures and groups.

Mencap website: www.mencap.org.uk

This is another well-constructed and informative website offering help and support for working with people who have learning difficulties.

Woodcock Ross, J (2011) *Specialist communication skills for social workers*. Basingstoke: Palgrave Macmillan.

This detailed book contains specialist chapters for working with particular groups of service-users. Particularly helpful are Chapter 3, Working with children, Chapter 8, Working with adults with disabilities, Chapter 9, Working with refugees and asylum seekers and Chapter 10, Working with older people.

Conclusion

The aim of this book has been to enable social workers to develop a range of counselling skills which will be useful in engagement with service-users. The main themes that I wish to emphasise in these concluding paragraphs are:

- the use of counselling skills in helping social workers to develop effective relationships with service-users;

- the importance of placing the service-user at the centre of decision making;

- the significance of social workers becoming aware of their own conscious and unconscious processes when working with service-users;

- how using particular counselling skills can serve to encourage sustainable change for service-users.

Using counselling skills to develop the social work relationship

Throughout this book there has been an emphasis on the importance of developing an effective working relationship with the service-user. Having a genuine interest in each service-user, wanting to engage, and striving to see each person as an individual are all necessary foundations for creating good working relationships. Service-users themselves tell us how much they value social workers who express warmth and respect and who offer space and support. Above all, service-users want their social workers to listen and to work collaboratively with them in finding solutions to their difficulties.

In this book, I have defined what constitutes effective listening skills and have explored particular techniques for listening well. These have included empathic responding where we try and put ourselves in the service-user's position and attempt to try and understand what the person might be thinking and feeling and why they may be behaving in a certain way. I have emphasised that while empathic responding is a difficult skill to achieve well, we need to strive to use it throughout every session with each service-user. There is a need to use empathic responding when forming relationships, when maintaining relationships, when challenging the person, during the process of finding out what is needed and in supporting the service-user through change.

Placing service-users at the centre of decision making

A key theme of this book is that when practitioners use counselling skills this can help service-users to take control of their own lives. Instead of telling someone what to do, we could say *what would help you most at the moment…* or *if nothing changes, what would your life look like in, say, six months from now?* Asking the right questions, which will help people to project themselves forward and think about the costs and consequences of making or not making changes, leaves the service-user in control of decision making rather than the practitioner. Many of the chapters have referred to and explored the Egan (2010) Skilled Helper model. Although this is used predominantly as a counselling model, it is also relevant to social work. The three stages of the model have been illustrated by their application to social work case studies. Using the model when engaging with service-users can help us to think: *what is happening to the person now, what do they want or need at this moment* and *how can I help them to get there?* Working in this way also keeps the service-user at the centre of the process and reduces the power of the practitioner.

Self-awareness when working with service-users

Self-awareness is a key component of social work and counselling training. If we can develop awareness of how we consciously and unconsciously engage with people then we will be better able to overcome barriers in our communication with service-users. Each chapter has included a number of activities which have invited you to explore your thinking, feelings and behaviour. *Tuning in* to service-users (Egan, 2010) requires practitioners to bring into conscious awareness that which is just out of reach. For example, in Chapter 4 we explored how having knowledge of ego-states from Transactional Analysis can help us to choose consciously from alternative forms of communication. Good supervision can help us to develop awareness of how we may be experienced by service-users and also helps us to engage more effectively. The more we understand ourselves, what motivates us, how and why we respond to each individual service-user as we do then the better we will be at remaining open, honest and congruent. Congruence, together with empathy and respect, deepens the social work relationship by developing trust.

Promoting change

Effective social workers uphold the worth and uniqueness of each service-user. Prizing the person (Rogers, 1961) in this way also means holding a fundamental belief that they have the capacity to change. Without this attitude, we would rapidly become cynical and dismissive towards service-users. If you have completed, engaged with and reflected on the counselling skills activities in this book, you may find that you have changed your approach to engagement with service-users in a number of areas. Change is not easy but reflecting on our own ability to change can help us to assist others to begin this process. Learning counselling skills that can help people to change or to make changes in their lives has been a key theme of this book. We have explored how to help service-users to recognise their own strengths; we have analysed skills which can help us to challenge service-users constructively. We have examined methods of encouraging people to set their own goals and also ways of supporting them to sustain change.

Building counselling skills into social work practice not only helps us in forming relationships, it also assists in those circumstances which require the assessment of risk and direct protective action. For example, empathic responses can encourage parents to disclose information in child protection cases. Using counselling skills to help parents and carers to self-assess the costs and consequences of continuing with a particular behaviour helps to place them in control of their own lives and potentially to bring about lasting changes.

A final point

I hope you have enjoyed this book and feel inspired to try out the models and skills that it contains. For me, developing expertise in using counselling skills requires constant practise and reflection. Each time I try to use an empathic response I wonder if I succeed in communicating back to the other person my desire to understand what they are saying directly and indirectly to me. Every time I engage with someone, I learn more about myself and my unconscious processes and how these might help or hinder our relationship. Using counselling skills is not easy but when we use them well it can be tremendously helpful and beneficial.

Reading a text about skills is never sufficient on its own to develop our proficiency so I urge you to practise the skills you have learned in this book and to reflect regularly on your progress. I hope you have found the chapters and activities useful and that they have helped you to develop your confidence in using counselling skills in social work.

Appendix 1 Professional Capabilities Framework

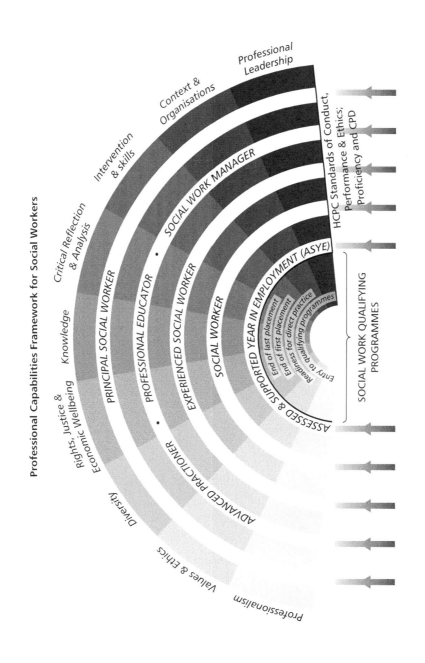

Professional Capabilities Framework for Social Workers

Professional Leadership

Context & Organisations

Intervention & Skills

Critical Reflection & Analysis

Knowledge

Rights, Justice & Economic Wellbeing

Diversity

Values & Ethics

Professionalism

PRINCIPAL SOCIAL WORKER

PROFESSIONAL EDUCATOR

EXPERIENCED SOCIAL WORKER

SOCIAL WORKER

ASSESSED & SUPPORTED YEAR IN EMPLOYMENT (ASYE)

SOCIAL WORK MANAGER

ADVANCED PRACTITIONER

End of last placement

End of first placement

Readiness for direct practice

Entry to qualifying programmes

HCPC Standards of Conduct, Performance & Ethics; Proficiency and CPD

SOCIAL WORK QUALIFYING PROGRAMMES

Appendix 2 Subject Benchmark for Social Work

5 Subject knowledge, understanding and skills

Subject knowledge and understanding

5.1 During their degree studies in social work, honours graduates should acquire, critically evaluate, apply and integrate knowledge and understanding in the following core areas of study.

5.1.1 Social work services, service users and carers, which include:

- the nature of social work services in a diverse society (with particular reference to concepts such as prejudice, interpersonal, institutional and structural discrimination, empowerment and anti-discriminatory practices);

- the nature and validity of different definitions of, and explanations for, the characteristics and circumstances of service users and the services required by them, drawing on knowledge from research, practice experience, and from service users and carers;

- the focus on outcomes, such as promoting the well-being of young people and their families, and promoting dignity, choice and independence for adults receiving services.

5.1.3 Values and ethics, which include:

- the moral concepts of rights, responsibility, freedom, authority and power inherent in the practice of social workers as moral and statutory agents;

5.1.4 Social work theory, which includes:

- research-based concepts and critical explanations from social work theory and other disciplines that contribute to the knowledge base of social work, including their distinctive epistemological status and application to practice;

- the relevance of psychological, physical and physiological perspectives to understanding personal and social development and functioning;

- social science theories explaining group and organisational behaviour, adaptation and change;

- models and methods of assessment, including factors underpinning the selection and testing of relevant information, the nature of professional judgement and the processes of risk assessment and decision-making;

- approaches and methods of intervention in a range of settings, including factors guiding the choice and evaluation of these;

- user-led perspectives.

5.1.5 The nature of social work practice, which includes:

- the nature and characteristics of skills associated with effective practice, both direct and indirect, with a range of service-users and in a variety of settings;

- the processes that facilitate and support service user choice and independence;

- the place of theoretical perspectives and evidence from international research in assessment and decision-making processes in social work practice;

- the integration of theoretical perspectives and evidence from international research into the design and implementation of effective social work intervention, with a wide range of service users, carers and others;

- the processes of reflection and evaluation, including familiarity with the range of approaches for evaluating service and welfare outcomes, and their significance for the development of practice and the practitioner.

Subject-specific skills and other skills

5.2 As an applied subject at honours degree level, social work necessarily involves the development of skills that may be of value in many situations (for example, analytical thinking, building relationships, working as a member of an organisation, intervention, evaluation and reflection). Some of these skills are specific to social work but many are also widely transferable. What helps to define the specific nature of these skills in a social work context are:

- the context in which they are applied and assessed (eg, communication skills in practice with people with sensory impairments or assessment skills in an interprofessional setting);

- the relative weighting given to such skills within social work practice (eg, the central importance of problem-solving skills within complex human situations);

- the specific purpose of skill development (eg, the acquisition of research skills in order to build a repertoire of research-based practice);

- a requirement to integrate a range of skills (ie, not simply to demonstrate these in an isolated and incremental manner).

5.3 All social work honours graduates should show the ability to reflect on and learn from the exercise of their skills. They should understand the significance of the concepts of continuing professional development and lifelong learning, and accept responsibility for their own continuing development.

Problem-solving skills

5.5 These are sub-divided into four areas.

5.5.1 Managing problem-solving activities: honours graduates in social work should be able to plan problem-solving activities, ie to:

- think logically, systematically, critically and reflectively;

- apply ethical principles and practices critically in planning problem-solving activities;

- plan a sequence of actions to achieve specified objectives, making use of research, theory and other forms of evidence;

- manage processes of change, drawing on research, theory and other forms of evidence.

5.5.3 Analysis and synthesis: honours graduates in social work should be able to analyse and synthesise knowledge gathered for problem-solving purposes, ie to:

- assess human situations, taking into account a variety of factors (including the views of participants, theoretical concepts, research evidence, legislation and organisational policies and procedures);

- consider specific factors relevant to social work practice (such as risk, rights, cultural differences and linguistic sensitivities, responsibilities to protect vulnerable individuals and legal obligations);

- critically analyse and take account of the impact of inequality and discrimination in work with people in particular contexts and problem situations.

5.5.4 Intervention and evaluation: honours graduates in social work should be able to use their knowledge of a range of interventions and evaluation processes selectively to:

- build and sustain purposeful relationships with people and organisations in community-based, and interprofessional contexts;

- make decisions, set goals and construct specific plans to achieve these, taking into account relevant factors including ethical guidelines;

- negotiate goals and plans with others, analysing and addressing in a creative manner human, organisational and structural impediments to change;

- implement plans through a variety of systematic processes that include working in partnership;

- undertake practice in a manner that promotes the well-being and protects the safety of all parties;

- engage effectively in conflict resolution;

- support service users to take decisions and access services, with the social worker as navigator, advocate and supporter;

- manage the complex dynamics of dependency and, in some settings, provide direct care and personal support in everyday living situations;

- meet deadlines and comply with external definitions of a task;

- plan, implement and critically review processes and outcomes;

- bring work to an effective conclusion, taking into account the implications for all involved;

- monitor situations, review processes and evaluate outcomes;

- use and evaluate methods of intervention critically and reflectively.

Communication skills

5.6 Honours graduates in social work should be able to communicate clearly, accurately and precisely (in an appropriate medium) with individuals and groups in a range of formal and informal situations, i.e. to:

- make effective contact with individuals and organisations for a range of objectives, by verbal, paper-based and electronic means;

- clarify and negotiate the purpose of such contacts and the boundaries of their involvement;

- listen actively to others, engage appropriately with the life experiences of service users, understand accurately their viewpoint and overcome personal prejudices to respond appropriately to a range of complex personal and interpersonal situations;

- use both verbal and non-verbal cues to guide interpretation;

- identify and use opportunities for purposeful and supportive communication with service users within their everyday living situations;

- follow and develop an argument and evaluate the viewpoints of, and evidence presented by, others;

- write accurately and clearly in styles adapted to the audience, purpose and context of the communication;

- use advocacy skills to promote others' rights, interests and needs;

- present conclusions verbally and on paper, in a structured form, appropriate to the audience for which these have been prepared;

- make effective preparation for, and lead meetings in a productive way;

- communicate effectively across potential barriers resulting from differences (for example, in culture, language and age).

Skills in working with others

5.7 Honours graduates in social work should be able to work effectively with others, ie to:

- involve users of social work services in ways that increase their resources, capacity and power to influence factors affecting their lives;

- consult actively with others, including service users and carers, who hold relevant information or expertise;

- act cooperatively with others, liaising and negotiating across differences such as organisational and professional boundaries and differences of identity or language;

- develop effective helping relationships and partnerships with other individuals, groups and organisations that facilitate change;

- act with others to increase social justice by identifying and responding to prejudice, institutional discrimination and structural inequality;

- act within a framework of multiple accountability (for example, to agencies, the public, service users, carers and others);

- challenge others when necessary, in ways that are most likely to produce positive outcomes.

Skills in personal and professional development

5.8 Honours graduates in social work should be able to:

- advance their own learning and understanding with a degree of independence;

- reflect on and modify their behaviour in the light of experience;

- identify and keep under review their own personal and professional boundaries;

- manage uncertainty, change and stress in work situations;

- handle inter and intrapersonal conflict constructively;

- understand and manage changing situations and respond in a flexible manner;

- challenge unacceptable practices in a responsible manner;

- take responsibility for their own further and continuing acquisition and use of knowledge and skills;

- use research critically and effectively to sustain and develop their practice.

Glossary

Active listening The process of listening to people and *demonstrating* that listening is taking place, by, for example, paraphrasing back to the service-user what has been heard.

Aphasia Loss of the ability to speak due to a brain injury or disease.

Asylum seeker A person who leaves their country of residence because of persecution for race, religion or political beliefs and who seeks refugee status in another nation.

Body language Non-verbal and often unconscious communication conveyed by, for example, our facial expressions and posture.

Clinical depression A severe form of depression which is not easily attributable to environmental factors or life events.

Collaborate To work alongside a service-user by finding out what they need and want and together identifying ways forward that will make a difference to their lives.

Counter-transference Unconscious processes and memories which are invoked in response to something that someone else says to us. For example, the service-user may remind us of someone significant in our own life and then we react to the person in a similar way.

Dissonance Where a person's views are self-conflicting, discordant or incongruous.

Egan Skilled Helper model A three-stage model developed by Gerard Egan (2010), which places service-users at the centre of decision making.

Empathy The process of trying to put ourselves in another person's position in an attempt to understand how they might be thinking, feeling or behaving. Empathy is not how we would feel if we were in the service-user's situation, it is about identifying what might be happening for the other person (Rogers, 1961).

Empowerment Fully involving service-users in *the formulation, implementation and evaluation of decisions determining the function and well-being of themselves and their wider environment* (Parrott, 2010, p42).

Mirroring Repeating back to the service-user what they have said using their exact words in order to highlight something of deep meaning (Clabby and O'Connor, 2004).

Paraphrasing Repeating back to the speaker the essence of what they have said using mainly our own choice of words (Hough, 1998).

Person-centred approach A way of engaging with clients devised by Carl Rogers (1961) where the helper works in a non-judgemental, empathic manner in order to help the service-user find their own solutions to their difficulties.

Personalisation This involves the introduction of personal budgets to give service-users as much control as possible over their own lives. It places people at the centre of a process which enables them to identify their needs and make choices about how they would like to live their lives (Carr, 2010).

Rapport Establishing a connection with a service-user where they feel understood, listened to and supported to find their own way forward.

Refugee A person who has been awarded the right to remain indefinitely or temporarily in a country to which they have sought asylum.

Strategy A plan of action which will assist in achieving a particular goal (Egan, 2010).

Supervision A process where an experienced practitioner offers guidance and support in the practice of social work to students and qualified social workers.

Therapeutic relationship A working alliance between the social worker and the service-user which brings about growth and change. According to Rogers (1961), a therapeutic relationship is one where the practitioner is genuine, accepting and understanding.

Transactional Analysis A theory of personality, communication and child development which helps people to better understand themselves and the ways in which they relate to others.

Transference A process where we unconsciously use our past experiences to shape our communication with others. For example, a service-user who has experienced a controlling parent may invite the social worker to be similarly dominant towards them.

Unconscious processes Often repressed memories and experiences from our past, which are relived in our current engagement with others without our conscious awareness of this happening (Casement, 1985).

References

Abrams, R (1999) *When parents die.* 2nd edition. London: Routledge.

Avis, M, Bulman, D and Leighton, P (2007) Factors affecting participation in Sure Start programmes: A qualitative investigation of parents' views. *Health and Social Care in the Community,* 15 (3): 203–11.

Axline, V (1964) *Dibs, in search of self.* London: Penguin.

Barna, LM (1994) Stumbling blocks in intercultural communication, in Samovar, LA and Porter, RE (eds) *Intercultural communication: A reader.* Boston, MA: Wadsworth Cengage Learning.

Barnes, J (2002) *Reform of social work education and training. Focus on the future. Key messages from focus groups about the future of social work training.* London: Department of Health. www.dh.gov.uk/en/Publicationsandstatistics/

Beresford, P, Croft, S and Adshead, L (2008) We don't see her as a social worker: A service user case study of the importance of the social worker's relationship and humanity. *British Journal of Social Work,* 38, 1388–407.

Berne, E (1964) *Games people play.* London: Penguin.

Berne, E (1971) *A layman's guide to psychiatry and psychoanalysis.* London: Penguin.

Berne, E (1975) *What do you say after you say hello?* London: Corgi.

Bethell, J and O'Sullivan, T (2010) *Diversity and difference SOW2005M, Open learning study block one, identity and working across difference.* Hull: University of Lincoln.

Borg, M and Kristiansen, K (2004) Recovery-oriented professionals: Helping relationships in mental health services. *Journal of Mental Health,* 13 (5): 493–505.

Brandes, D (1979) *Gamesters' handbook: 140 games for teachers and group leaders.* London: Hutchinson.

Bridges, W (1991) *Managing transitions: Making the most of change.* Cambridge, MA: Perseus Books.

Brown, A (1994) *Groupwork.* 3rd edition. Aldershot: Arena.

Burgess, R (2005) A model for enhancing individual and organisational learning of 'emotional intelligence': The drama and winner's triangles. *Social Work Education,* 24 (1): 97–112.

Caris-Verhallen, WMCN, Kerkstra, A and Bensing, JM (1999) Non-verbal behaviour in nurse–elderly patient communication. *Journal of Advanced Nursing,* 29 (4): 808–18.

Carr, S (2010) Personalisation: A rough guide (revised edition). London: Social Care Institute for Excellence, www.scie.org.uk/publications/reports

Casement, P (1985) *On learning from the patient.* London: Routledge.

Clabby, J and O'Connor, R (2004) Teaching learners to use mirroring: Rapport lessons from neurolinguistic programming. *Family Medicine,* 36 (8): 541–3.

Connor, M (1994) *Training the counsellor: An integrative approach.* London: Routledge.

Currer, C (2007) *Loss and social work.* Exeter: Learning Matters.

de Board, R (1997) *Counselling for toads.* London: Routledge.

Deci, EL and Ryan RM (2002) *Handbook of self-determination research.* Woodbridge: Boydell and Brewer.

Department for Children, Schools and Families, Department of Health and the Department of Business, Innovation and Skills in partnership with the Social Work Reform Board (2010) *Building a safe and confident future: Implementing the recommendations of the Social Work Task Force.* London: Stationery Office. www.dh.gov.uk/en/publicationsandstatistics/

Dickson, A (1982) *A woman in your own right.* London: Quartet.

Dickson, A (2000) *Women at work: Strategies for survival and success.* London: Kogan.

Doel, M (2006) *Using groupwork.* Abingdon: Routledge.

Doran, GT (1981) There's a S.M.A.R.T. way to write management's goals and objectives. *Management Review,* 70 (11): 35–6.

Dyregrov, A (1991) *Grief in children: A handbook for adults.* London: Jessica Kingsley.

Egan, G (1977) *You and me: The skills of communicating and relating to others.* Belmont, CA: Wadsworth.

Egan, G (1994) *The skilled helper: A problem management approach to helping.* 5th edition. Pacific Grove, CA: Brooks/Cole.

Egan, G (1996) *Many faces of both bereavement and counselling.* Lecture, Hull University, 7th October 1996.

Egan, G (2010) *The skilled helper: A problem management and opportunity development approach to helping.* 9th edition. Belmont, CA: Brooks/Cole.

Faulkner, A (1998) *When the news is bad: A guide for health professionals.* Cheltenham: Stanley Thornes.

Fook, J (2002) *Social work: Critical theory and practice.* London: Sage.

Forrester, D, Kershaw, S, Moss, H and Hughes, L (2008) Communication skills in child protection: how do social workers talk to parents? *Child and Family Social Work,* 13 (1): 41–51.

Freud, S (1916) Lecture 7: The manifest content of dreams and the latent dream-thoughts, in Strachey, J and Richards, A (1973) (eds) *Freud: 1. Introductory lectures on psychoanalysis.* Reading: Pelican.

Geldard, G and Geldard, D (2009) *Relationship counselling for children, young people and families.* London: Sage.

General Social Care Council (2004) *Code of practice for social care workers.* London: General Social Care Council.

Gilbert, H, Rose, D and Slade, M (2008) The importance of relationships in mental health care: A qualitative study of service users' experiences of psychiatric hospital admission in the UK. *BMC Health Services Research,* 8 (92): 1–12.

Goldbart, J and Caton, S (2010) *Communication and people with the most complex needs: What works and why this is essential.* Manchester: Research Insitute for Health and Social Change, Manchester Metropolitan University. www.mencap.org.uk

Hanna, F, Hanna, CA and Keys, SA (1999) Fifty strategies for counselling defiant, aggressive adolescents: Reaching, accepting and relating. *Journal of Counselling and Development,* 77 (4): 395–405.

Harris, TA (1973) *I'm ok – you're ok.* London: Pan.

Hawkins, P and Shohet, R (2007) *Supervision in the helping professions.* 3rd edition. Buckingham: Open University Press.

Help the Aged (2007) *Consulting and engaging with older people. Dos and don'ts.* London: Age UK Online. www.ageuk.org.uk

Hewson, J (1990) *Ego-states lecture.* TA 101 course. London.

Hough, M (1998) *Counselling skills and theory.* London: Hodder and Stoughton.

Hough, M (2001) *Groupwork skills and theory.* London: Hodder and Stoughton.

Houston, G (1990) *The red book of groups.* 3rd edition. Norfolk: The Rochester Foundation.

Jacobs, M (2005) *The presenting past: The core of psychodynamic counselling and therapy.* 3rd edition. Buckingham: Open University Press.

Jacobs, M (2010) *Psychodynamic counselling in action.* 4th edition. London: Sage.

Jeffers, S (2007) *Feel the fear and do it anyway, 20th anniversary edition: How to turn your fear and indecision into confidence and action.* London: Vermilion.

Karpman, S (1968) Fairy tales and script drama analysis. *Transactional Analysis Bulletin,* 7 (26): 39–43.

Kastenbaum, R (2000) *The psychology of death.* 3rd edition. London: Free Association Books.

Kiessling, J, Pichora-Fuller, MK, Gatehouse, S, Arlinger, S, Chisolm, T, Davis, AC, Erber, NP, Hickson, L, Holmes, A, Rosenhall, U and von Wedel, H (2003) Candidature for and delivery of audiological services: Special needs of older people. *International Journal of Audiology*, 42 (2): 92–101.

Koprowska, J (2003) The right kind of telling? Locating the teaching of interviewing skills within a systems framework. *British Journal of Social Work,* 33: 291–308.

Koprowska, J (2010) *Communication and interpersonal skills in social work.* 3rd edition. Exeter: Learning Matters.

Kubler-Ross, E (1973) *On death and dying.* London: Routledge.

Lefevre, M (2010) *Communicating with children and young people.* Bristol: The Policy Press.

Lindsay, T (2009) *Social work intervention.* Exeter: Learning Matters.

Lindsay, T and Orton, S (2011) *Groupwork practice in social work.* 2nd edition. Exeter: Learning Matters.

Lishman, J (2009) *Communication in social work.* 2nd edition. Basingstoke: Palgrave Macmillan.

Lombard, D (2010) Social care staff run high risk of assault, new figures reveal. *Community Care,* 19th November, 2010.

Lombard, D, Hicks, J and Riggall, S (2010) How to say goodbye. *Community Care,* 28th October, 2010.

McBride (1998) *The assertive social worker.* Aldershot: Arena.

McGoldrick, M, Gerson, R and Petry, S (2008) *Genograms: Assessment and intervention.* 3rd edition. London: WW Norton & Co.

McGregor, K (2010) Violence against social care staff – Community Care special report. *Community Care,* 5th May, 2010.

McKelley, RA (2007) Men's resistance to seeking help: Using individual psychology to understand counselling-reluctant men. *Journal of Individual Psychology,* 63 (1): 48–58.

Mantell, A (2009) *Social work skills with adults.* Exeter: Learning Matters.

Mearns, D (1997) *Person-centred counselling training.* London: Sage.

Millar, S (2006) *CALL centre communication passport template.* Edinburgh: University of Edinburgh. www.communicationpassports.org.uk

Miller, L (2006) *Counselling skills for social work.* London: Sage.

Milner, J and O'Byrne, P (2009) *Assessment in social work.* 3rd edition. Basingstoke: Palgrave Macmillan.

Moss, B (2008) *Communication skills for health and social care.* London: Sage.

Munro, E (2011) *The Munro review of child protection: Final report: A child-centred system.* London: The Stationery Office. www.education.gov.uk/publications/

National Council for Hospice and Specialist Palliative Care Services (2003) *Breaking bad news… Regional guidelines.* Belfast: Department of Health, Social Services and Public Safety. www.dhsspsni.gov.uk/

Nelson-Jones, R (2008) *Basic counselling skills: A helper's manual.* 2nd edition. London: Sage.

Oliver, B and Pitt, R (2011) *Working with children, young people and families: A course book for foundation degrees.* Exeter: Learning Matters.

O'Sullivan, T (1994) *Social work with and within groups.* London: The Open Learning Foundation.

O'Sullivan, T (2011) *Decision making in social work.* 2nd edition. Basingstoke: Palgrave Macmillan.

Oxford English Dictionary (2009) 11th edition. Oxford: OUP.

Parrott, L (2010) *Values and ethics in social work practice.* 2nd edition. Exeter: Learning Matters.

Payne, S, Horn, S and Relf, M (1999) *Loss and bereavement.* Buckingham: Open University Press.

Preston-Shoot, M (2007) *Effective groupwork.* 2nd edition. Basingstoke: Palgrave Macmillan.

Quackenbush, R (2008) The use of modern psychoanalytic techniques in the treatment of children and adolescents. *Modern Psychoanalysis,* 33 (2): 88–101.

Rew, M and Ferns, T (2005) A balanced approach to dealing with violence and aggression at work. *British Journal of Nursing,* 14 (4): 227–32.

Richards, S, Ruch, G and Trevithick, P (2005) Communication skills training for practice: The ethical dilemma for social work education. *Social Work Education,* 24 (4): 409–22.

Rogers, C (1961) *On becoming a person: A therapist's view of psychotherapy.* London: Constable.

Scott, M and Stradling, S (2006) *Counselling for post-traumatic stress disorder.* 3rd edition. London: Sage.

Scrutton, S (1996) What can you expect, my dear, at my age? *Bereavement Care,* 15 (3): 28–9.

Smith, MJ (1975) *When I say no I feel guilty: How to cope, using the skills of systematic assertive therapy.* New York: Bantam.

Stewart, I (1989) *Transactional analysis counselling in action.* London: Sage.

Stewart, I and Joines, V (1987) *TA today: A new introduction to transactional analysis.* Nottingham: Lifespace Publishing.

Stroebe, M and Schut, H (1999) The dual process model of coping with bereavement: Rationale and description. *Death Studies,* 23 (3): 197–224.

Stuart-Hamilton, I (2011) Introduction, in Stuart-Hamilton, I (ed) *An introduction to gerontology.* Cambridge: Cambridge University Press.

Sugarman, L (1995) Action man: An interview with Gerard Egan. *British Journal of Guidance and Counselling,* 33 (2): 275–87.

Sutherland, S and Stroots, S (2010) The impact of participation in an inclusive adventure education trip on group dynamics. *Journal of Leisure Research,* 42 (1): 153–76.

Taylor, B (1998) *Working with others: Helping, counselling and human relations.* Wetherby: Oasis Publications.

Taylor, BJ (2011) *Working with aggression and resistance in social work.* Exeter: Learning Matters.

Thompson, N (2000) *Understanding social work.* Basingstoke: Palgrave.

Thorne, B (1990) Person-centred therapy, in Dryden, W (ed) *Individual therapy.* Milton Keynes: Open University Press.

Trevithick, P, Richards, S, Rush, G and Moss, B (2004) *Knowledge review 06: Teaching and learning communication skills in social work education.* London: Social Care Institute for Excellence. www.scie.org.uk/publications/

Tuckman, B (1965) Developmental sequence in small groups. *Psychological Bulletin,* 63 (6): 384–99.

Tuckman, B and Jensen, M (1977) Stages of small-group development revisited. *Group Organization Management,* 2 (4): 419–27.

Warren, J (2007) *Service user and carer participation in social work.* Exeter: Learning Matters.

Watts, R and Garza, Y (2008) Using children's drawings to facilitate the acting 'as if' technique. *Journal of Individual Psychology,* 64 (1): 113–18.

Whittaker, DS (1985) *Using groups to help people.* London: Routledge and Kegan Paul.

Williams, P (2009) *Social work with people with learning difficulties.* Exeter: Learning Matters.

Winston's Wish (Undated) *Supporting a bereaved child or young person. A guide for parents and carers.* Cheltenham: Winston's Wish. www.winstonswish.org.uk

Woodcock Ross, J (2011) *Specialist communication skills for social workers.* Basingstoke: Palgrave MacMillan.

Woodcock Ross, J and Tregaskis, C (2008) Understanding structural and communication barriers to ordinary family life for families with disabled children: A combined social work and social model of disability analysis. *British Journal of Social Work,* 38 (1): 55–71.

Worden, JW (1991) *Grief counselling and grief therapy: A handbook for the mental health practitioner.* 2nd edition. London: Routledge.

Wosket, V (2006) *Egan's skilled helper model: Developments and applications in counselling.* Hove: Routledge.

Index